Level Up!
CREATIVE COSPLAY

Costume Design & Creation, SFX Makeup, LED Basics & More

T0277129

FanPowered PRESS
an imprint of C&T Publishing

Text copyright © 2022 by Amanda Haas

Photography © 2022 by Amanda Haas, unless otherwise noted

Artwork copyright © 2022 by C&T Publishing, Inc.

PUBLISHER: Amy Barrett-Daffin

CREATIVE DIRECTOR: Gailen Runge

SENIOR EDITOR: Roxane Cerda

EDITOR: Beth Baumgartel and Roxane Cerda

COVER/BOOK DESIGNER: April Mostek

PRODUCTION COORDINATOR: Tim Manibusan

ILLUSTRATOR: Aliza Shalit

PHOTO ASSISTANT: Gabriel Martinez

COVER PHOTOGRAPHY by Alexandra Lee Studios

COSPLAY PHOTOGRAPHY by Alex Brumley of Alexandra Lee Studios,
unless otherwise noted. Noted photographers retain copyright of their images.

Published by FanPowered Press, an imprint of C&T Publishing, Inc., P.O. Box 1456,
Lafayette, CA 94549

All rights reserved. No part of this work covered by the copyright hereon may be used in any form or
reproduced by any means—graphic, electronic, or mechanical, including photocopying, recording,
taping, or information storage and retrieval systems—without written permission from the publisher.
The copyrights on individual artworks are retained by the artists as noted in *Level Up! Creative
Cosplay* These designs may be used to make items for personal use only and may not be used for
the purpose of personal profit. Items created to benefit nonprofit groups, or that will be publicly
displayed, must be conspicuously labeled with the following credit: "Designs copyright © 2022 by
Amanda Haas from the book *Level Up! Creative Cosplay* from C&T Publishing, Inc." Permission for all
other purposes must be requested in writing from C&T Publishing, Inc.

Attention Teachers: C&T Publishing, Inc., encourages the use of our books as texts for teaching. You
can find lesson plans for many of our titles at ctpub.com or contact us at ctinfo@ctpub.com.

We take great care to ensure that the information included in our products is accurate and presented
in good faith, but no warranty is provided, nor are results guaranteed. Having no control over the
choices of materials or procedures used, neither the author nor C&T Publishing, Inc., shall have
any liability to any person or entity with respect to any loss or damage caused directly or indirectly
by the information contained in this book. For your convenience, we post an up-to-date listing of
corrections on our website (ctpub.com). If a correction is not already noted, please contact our
customer service department at ctinfo@ctpub.com or P.O. Box 1456, Lafayette, CA 94549.

Trademark (™) and registered trademark (®) names are used throughout this book. Rather than use
the symbols with every occurrence of a trademark or registered trademark name, we are using the
names only in the editorial fashion and to the benefit of the owner, with no intention of infringement.

Library of Congress Cataloging-in-Publication Data

Names: Haas, Amanda Dawn, 1988- author.

Title: Level up! Creative cosplay : costume design & creation, SFX makeup,

LED basics & more / by Amanda Haas.

Other titles: Creative cosplay

Description: Lafayette, CA : FanPowered Press, an imprint of C&T

Publishing, Inc., [2022] | Summary: "Includes an in-depth look into

patterning and design, fabric information on specialty fabrics,

stabilizers, painting, dyeing and more. Creative Cosplay, helps newer

cosplayers add new skills and advance their skill sets with steady

guidance that takes them from their sketchbook to the convention floor

and beyond"-- Provided by publisher.

Identifiers: LCCN 2022021389 | ISBN 9781644032190 (trade paperback) | ISBN

9781644032206 (ebook)

Subjects: LCSH: Costume design. | Cosplay--Equipment and supplies. |

Handicraft. | Wearable technology.

Classification: LCC TT633 .H3325 2022 | DDC 746.9/2--dc23/eng/20220705

LC record available at https://lccn.loc.gov/2022021389

10 9 8 7 6 5 4 3 2 1

DEDICATION

Special thanks to Regan and Casey—without our daily chats about writing our books together, I wouldn't have been able to finish this book!

Another special (but weird) thank you to Alex Brumley's family condo, aka "The Sand Crib." If it wasn't for The Crib getaway, this book might not have been written.

ACKNOWLEDGMENTS

My biggest thanks go to Alex Brumley of Alexandra Lee Studios for again providing most of the photos for this book. I'm honored to feature her work along with the cosplay art created by the folks in the photos. Alex always has a way of combining incredible Photoshop work with incredible cosplays. I can't wait to create more art with her!

I also want to thank Beth Baumgartel and the team at C&T Publishing. I can't thank you all enough for giving me the confidence to write my second book with your company.

CONTENTS

INTRODUCTION

In 2011, I visited my first comic con. It was a small one: Derby City Comic Con in Louisville, Kentucky, to be exact. It was just one big room with space for a dealer's hall and the related panels. I wore a handmade *Star Wars* skirt, shirt, and Rebellion symbol necklace. I thought I was dressed for the con, but it turned out I was so underdressed. I saw fully-outfitted Stormtroopers, X-Men cosplay groups, and multiple *Mortal Kombat* characters in full costumes. My fashion items were cute, but I knew that I needed to be a cosplayer. I'll never forget that distinct moment and, honestly, that is when the light went on for me. I started reading about cosplay, sewing up some outfits, and learning about working with wigs. It was that drive and passion that led me to keep learning about the skills I needed to pull off the looks I wanted. This journey is never-ending and is always exciting.

Learning new skills and expanding your knowledge on how to make cosplays is invigorating. It's the main reason I wrote this book! I hope it helps you in your continued journey of all things cosplay. You've likely already made a few costumes and are ready to expand your skill set and really take your costumes to the next level. Between these covers you'll find information on advanced sewing options, cosplay makeup, adding lights to your costumes, and much more.

COSPLAYER: Jedimanda
COSTUME: Kitana from *Mortal Kombat 3*
The first cosplay that I wore to a convention, 2012

COSPLAYER: Jedimanda
COSTUME: Darth Maul from the Star Wars franchise
The first non–Halloween cosplay I made. I wore it to the 2011 3D rerelease of *Star Wars Episode 1: The Phantom Menace*

DESIGNING YOUR COSPLAYS

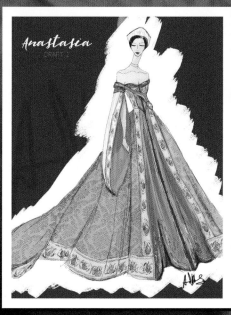

An early sketch, inspired by the animation in the 1997 movie *Anastasia*. I toned down the colors in the gown to make it read more royal.

COSPLAYER: Jedimanda
COSTUME: Princess Anastasia from *Anastasia*
The finished cosplay after several revisions and drafts

Inspired by Grogu from *The Mandalorian*, I drafted a grown-up feminine version of the costume

I knew when I started cosplaying that I wanted to design my own costumes. Even with my college-level garment design background and sewing technique classes, I was still nervous about how to bring a design from paper to the real world. My first college project was an interesting bodice top with a weird peplum.

I designed it, drafted it, and made a pattern with odd seamlines, and needless to say, it did not work! I'm so glad it didn't work, though, because it taught me an important lesson—that it's okay to go back into a drafted pattern and rework the design. After all, if you don't make mistakes, how do you learn? Drafting and designing can be intimidating but don't be afraid to jump in and discover, and more importantly, don't be afraid to start over and try again because that is how you will learn!

COSPLAYER: Jedimanda
COSTUME: Grogu from *The Mandalorian*
Photo by David Ngo

Why Go for Originality?

In my opinion, designing and creating your own cosplay is the ultimate achievement in this weird costuming world. I truly love the ability to draw something and know that I can transform that two-dimensional design into a three-dimensional world. It brings me such joy to be able to share my design process for making an original costume—it's just so fun.

Before we dive into how to start designing our own cosplays, I want to touch on the topic of sharing your original designs online. I think everyone knows that not all folks on the internet are nice and that they might (or might not) credit you if they decide to make the costume you've just designed for yourself. You post the design online to show everyone, and suddenly someone copies your design and makes it. Unfortunately, it does happen, so when you share your designs online, just remember to add a statement that you don't want anyone to claim ownership of the design but that you are fine with people making it for their own enjoyment. Maybe add a watermark as well. Sometimes those small statements will deter people from stealing your design idea.

COSPLAYER: Jedimanda
COSTUME: Spooky dress, original design

Cosplay Sketchbook

I usually complete sketches before I start my projects and they help keep me on track with materials and timeline.

I want to introduce you to my cosplay sketchbook. This sketchbook is my starting point for all my cosplays. Before I begin planning, I try my best to write, draw, and list all the materials, garments, accessories, and relevant information that I need to make the cosplay.

This sketch kept me on track by noting commercial patterns that could be used as starting points and a couple of key accessories that I had to source.

For this jumping-off point, I always include my end deadline, the basic fabrics I will need, any accessories I'll need to source or make, and any additional notes such as commercial pattern numbers, or pieces that will take a long time to make and should be prioritized. I like to make my journal pretty, but a more utilitarian approach would work just as well. The small sketches of the garments help me establish the basic lines of the garments I will need, whether that is a princess seam or a bell sleeve, sketching helps me figure that aspect out from the beginning.

In addition to keeping me organized and inspired, this starting sketch reminded me that the helmet was priority number one, but that I already had a prop blaster that could be used for this cosplay.

A sketchbook isn't something that everyone makes, but it's a great first step. You can take your time to create a fun layout and just let all your ideas flow out. You can also put a small sketch in to start to build your vision for the final cosplay by establishing seam lines, fabric choices in terms of texture and pattern, and garment types. These original sketches also help me identify if my envisioned garment is a design that already exists or something you are tweaking a little bit, in which case I might be able to use or start with a commercial pattern. Doing small idea sketches first, here in the sketchbook, helps your creative brain form a road map to beginning the design.

Cosplay Progress Journal

In addition to a sketchbook, keeping a cosplay progress journal is also important, especially if you decide to compete with your cosplay in costume competitions. Besides the fact that a progress journal helps keep you on budget and your design in line with your plans, the cosplay judges will probably ask for one.

You can use a sketchbook with printed photos placed within it, or you can create a series of printable PDFs and store the pages in a binder—it's up to you! Make sure you include plenty of work-in-progress photos with captions about what you were doing and what you used. Don't overthink a work-in-progress photo: Use your phone and snap plenty of photos during every step of your creative journey. Judges love to see photos of the items you made that they don't see at first, like undergarments, shoes, or handmade suits that are worn under armor. A cosplay progress journal doesn't have to be super long; it should just be a great walk through your cosplay.

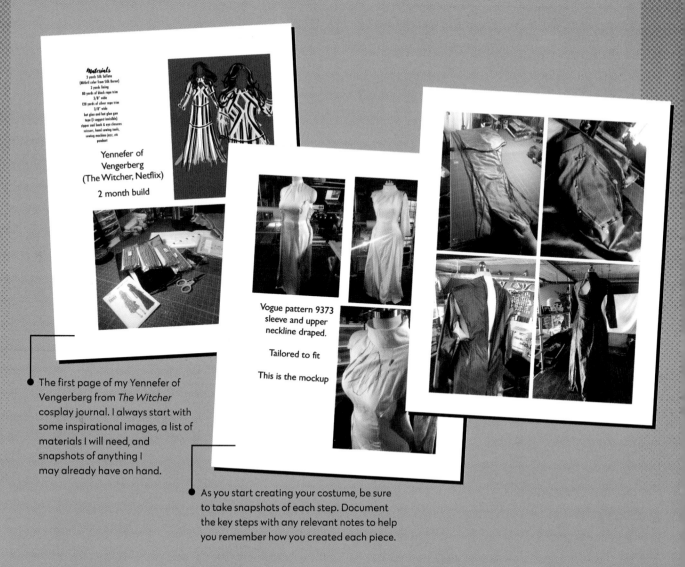

The first page of my Yennefer of Vengerberg from *The Witcher* cosplay journal. I always start with some inspirational images, a list of materials I will need, and snapshots of anything I may already have on hand.

As you start creating your costume, be sure to take snapshots of each step. Document the key steps with any relevant notes to help you remember how you created each piece.

Sketching clothing might seem intimidating at first, but if you follow the steps in this chapter and give it a bit of practice, you'll be sketching like a pro in no time

Drawing a Fashion Croquis

A croquis (pronounced kroh-kee) is a basic sketch of the body used in fashion design. It's one of the first skills you learn in clothing design school (or you can teach yourself with my step-by-step instructions!). I learned how to draw them in school during my costuming courses, and I believe they are super handy for learning the proper way to sketch a body for clothing design. A croquis serves as a blank canvas that you can use over and over again to create numerous costume designs.

First, decide if you want to draw digitally or traditionally (i.e., with a pencil and paper). I do both: Some days I feel like digital drawing, and other days I love to get all my sketching materials and go to town in my sketchbook. It's up to you; there is no right way.

For this tutorial, however, I'm going to show you how to draw a basic croquis with a pencil, ruler, paper, and a marker. We are going to learn the *nine head croquis* sketch. (That's the technical term if you want to do a bit more research.) Let's get to sketching. You will need a ruler (preferably a 12″ standard ruler), a pencil, a marker, and two pieces of white paper.

1. Divide the paper in half vertically and draw a line down the middle with your ruler.

2. Drop about a quarter of an inch from the top edge of the paper and mark a dot on the vertical line. This mark is "zero."

3. From the "zero" mark, measure 1″ down and make another dot mark on the line.

4. Continue down the paper until you reach your ninth mark.

5. Starting at the second dot from the top, draw a horizontal line through the dot. This will start to section off the paper into the *nine heads*. Continue to draw horizontal lines through each dot. Number those lines from one to nine on the left side of the paper. **A**

6. Label the lines on the right side in this order:

LINE 1: (leave blank)	**LINE 4:** hips	**LINE 7:** calves
LINE 2: apex/bust	**LINE 5:** thighs	**LINE 8:** ankles
LINE 3: waist/elbow	**LINE 6:** knees	**LINE 9:** floor

7. In the first section, draw a head starting at the top dot, with the second dot being the bottom chin point so that it is 1˝ long. The head should be about ¾˝ wide.

8. Draw the neck so that it extends about halfway down between line 1 and line 2 (still on the vertical line). Then draw the shoulders, which should slope slightly but not much. The width of the shoulders should be about 1¾˝. Draw a horizontal line to connect the shoulder points. **B**

9. The waist is next. On line 3, measure and mark dots equidistant from the center line and 1⅛˝ apart; draw the waistline connecting the two dots. Don't worry if your body size is different. We make alterations at the end to match our body sizes.

10. Connect the shoulder points to the ends of the newly drawn waistline. Now you have a torso!

11. Add in bust drawings if you'd like at this point. They are drawn just slightly under line 2. **C**

12. Hip time! The hips should be the same width as the shoulder line, which is 1¾˝. Use your ruler to draw a light vertical line from both shoulder points down to line 4. Then draw a curved line from each side of the waist to the hip points on line 4.

13. Mark a small crotch line about ⅛˝ down from line 4 on the main vertical line.

14. On line 6, draw a circle on both sides of the central vertical line to represent knees.

A The lines begin to section your paper into the various sections of the body

B Use a ruler to ensure your dimensions are correct and do not slope the shoulders too much

C Before adding in hips, add a bust if desired

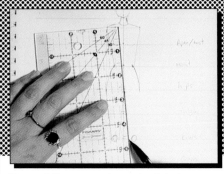

D Carefully connect the inside of the knee circles to the crotch line

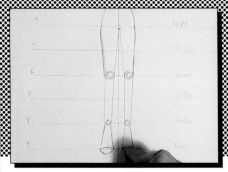

E Adding the curved shape to the bottom of your trapezoid results in realistic feet shapes

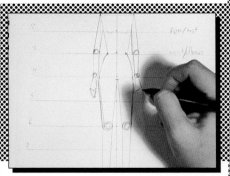

F Repeat the steps to drawing a foot to add realistic hand shapes

G Going over the sketched lines with a permanent marker

15. Connect the outside hip lines to the outer part of the knee circles. Connect the crotch line to the inner edges of the circles. And now the croquis has thighs! **D**

16. Draw ankles, much like the knees on line 8.

17. Connect the knee circles to the ankle circles as in step 15. I recommend veering out a bit as you pass line 7 to mimic the shape of your calves.

18. Next, it's time to draw feet. The easiest way is to draw trapezoids connected to the ankles, but slightly wider and slightly curved, from line 8 to line 9. Below line 9 draw a slightly shaped half-circle below each trapezoid for the toes, and you have a simple pair of shoes. **E**

19. Almost finished—time to add some arms. Draw a circle on the outer part of each lighter vertical line that you drew on line 3 to help connect the shoulders to hips.

20. Connect the shoulder point to the outside edge of each elbow circle Then draw a line from line 2 to the inner edge of the elbow circle. The upper arm is done!

21. Starting at line 4 and just a bit outside and beyond the hip curve on each side of the croquis, draw a small circle to mark the wrists.

22. Connect the elbows to the wrists with straight lines.

23. Last, draw the hands between lines 4 and 5. As with the feet, I find that a trapezoid shape is easiest to work with here. **F**

24. If desired, add facial features. You've just finished your sketch! Now let's finish the croquis.

25. Here is where you can alter your sketch to better fit your body type. I'll use my body as an example: My hips and thighs are wider, so I will adjust the hip curves a bit here and maybe bring my inner thighs closer together too. I'll widen my upper arms and chest a bit so that it looks more like me!

26. Grab your marker and reinforce the lines you'll need for your designs, particularly the body shape lines, and I like to draw the bust, waist, and hip horizontal lines too. Your croquis is now finished! **G**

Using a Fashion Croquis

Okay, so how do you use a croquis? Well, it's easy! Lay a blank piece of paper over the croquis and trace the lines you need for your sketch. It's so simple! The more practice you have drawing these lines, the more comfortable you will be shaping the body differently or contorting the angles to better sketch the various features of your design. The original croquis is your basic body template, and you just keep tracing it to draw your cosplay designs.

TIP

I know some of you might be thinking, what about a more masculine or male form? Or maybe a back view sketch? Sure! These are easy adjustments to make to your basic croquis. You might want to trace multiple copies of the basic croquis before you ink and reinforce the lines.

For male croquis, make the chest and waist wider and the hips smaller.

For a back view sketch, use the original croquis but with a blank head or add hair rather than facial features. Remove the bustlines, knees, ankles, elbows, and wrist circles. You'll need to redraw your hands by redrawing the trapezoids, but reversed and replacing the original feet trapezoids with smaller shapes to represent a heel. Round out these edges to get a more realistic or natural form.

Drawing Fabric and Coloring on a Croquis

Now the real designing begins. Drawing fabric on a croquis is all about experimenting and practice. A lot depends on what you are drawing and on how much erasing and then inking you'll do. I know when I draw big ball gowns, I focus on the shape around the hips, the seamlines on the bodice, and the drape of the fabric and how to show it. Remember to refer to your sketchbook and progress journal for guidance.

My watercolor palette set with paintbrush, water brush pens, a mechanical pencil, and a Micron pen (my favorite inking pen)

1. The first consideration is whether the main fabric will be light and airy or stiff and heavy. This decision helps determine where to add design lines and how the garments are shaped. Bolder lines can imply a heavier fabric where lighter strokes and lots of movement suggest a lighter fabric. A higher opacity of your color can also suggest depth within the folds of the fabric or thicker and more plush fabrics where a more translucent color can indicate a more sheer or airy fabric. **A**

A When sketching my Grogu-inspired costume I used heavier lines to indicate the garment outline on the top but at the bottom they suggest a heavier fabric. I also used multiple tones of the same khaki color to indicate deeper shadows, showing fabric weight.

2. Next you need to decide where to place the *seamlines*. Seamlines are the lines along which the different pieces of fabric will be sewn together to create the shape of the finished garment. These are often places like the neckline, where a sleeve joins the bodice, along the side of a bodice, or at your natural waist, to name just a few. They are the lines along which fabric pieces are joined together to create a garment. I believe that, aside from color selection, the placement of the seamlines is the most important aspect of designing from scratch. The seamlines are your maps, added at the area of the garment that you want to be the center of attention. The seamlines help you select a pattern if you decide to start with a commercial pattern (see Using a Commercial Pattern, page 26). Or the seamlines provide a starting point if you decide to drape your cosplay on a dress form. Sometimes, if the torso area has a lot of seam work, I'll make a separate and bigger sketch of that area. It is a good idea to sketch any area that has a lot of design details, so you have a clear reference. So grab a light pencil and make your marks. This sketch is your own—your creation—and you do not have to adhere to any existing style or look. **B**

B Drawing seam lines for a simple skirt. Adding the darker lines indicates that to get the look I want, I will need to make a multipanel skirt.

Some of my favorite books on traditional sewing

TIP

If you are curious about traditional seam work in clothing, the internet is your best friend. And if you can, visit a library and borrow some books on fashion design. These books show basic sketches of common clothing. You'll learn about princess seams, boat necks, and all kinds of other fashion terms and design options.

3. Once you have sketched the important seam-lines, it's time to color your design. You may have some colors or fabric choices already in mind from your original sketchbook design and you can just color in the tones you need. If you have more color options you can make digital palettes or separate watercolor pages of practice color choices. You can then choose the one you like best and add it to your actual sketch.

I sometimes use Procreate on my iPad to help select my final colors. Sketching digitally allows me to try lots of options without damaging my original sketch or having to erase.

DIGITAL COLORING I find it easier to color my sketches digitally because most programs give you the ability to layer colors and add texture easily. You can also play around with all the different brushes and layering options to quickly change colors, line weights, and try out various options without having to revise the whole sketch or start over from the beginning. Applications like Procreate and Adobe Illustrator are fantastic programs to use for digital sketching.

TRADITIONAL COLORING If you are using traditional sketching methods, try coloring your sketches with watercolors. Watercolors are a great way to layer color and show tones. Remember to not use too much water, make the layers light, and let each layer dry before adding another. Watercoloring in layers is the key to developing the look and feel of your fabric. It takes practice, but it's an easy way to establish the color and any obvious pattern in your chosen fabric.

My original design sketch of Mobius from *Loki*. I now have a good sense of the shape of the garments, my seamlines, the fabrics I'll need, and the fabric colors.

Layering really helped me define the depth of the garment and to establish the pattern in the fabric.

Stay True to Yourself

To wrap up this design chapter, I want you to remember a couple of things.

One, be honest with yourself. When you are drawing a custom or original costume for yourself, you want it to represent you and your body on the page. So even though a super tall and rail-thin model may look nice and "fashiony" on the page, I know that's not me. So make sure your basic croquis represents your body.

Two, nothing is ever permanent. Don't be afraid to make many copies of your design idea. You know how to make a standard basic croquis, and from there, your design copies can be infinite.

Three, experiment! Get weird with your seamlines. Draw out ideas that might not work, but try them to see if they do. Research patterns and traditional clothing design, and blend ideas together. This is your imagination; this is your design. Have fun.

NADJA

My digital sketch of Nadja from *What We Do in the Shadows*

COSPLAYER: Jedimanda
COSTUME: Nadja from *What We Do in the Shadows*
You can see how the original sketches helped me envision the finished costume.

PATTERNING

In this chapter, we dive deeper into what makes a costume, including the anatomy of a costume, the importance of accurate measurements, and whether to adapt a commercial pattern or make your own. Let's start with the anatomy of a costume.

COSPLAYER: Jedimanda
COSTUME: Yennefer of Vengerberg from *The Witcher*

COSPLAYER: Jedimanda
COSTUME: Doctor Strange from Marvel Cinematic Universe
This costume consists of a tunic, a vest, pants, belts, corset, armbands, boots, necklace, and a cape
Photo by World of Gwendana

Costume Anatomy

A costume is, by definition, a set of clothes in a style typical of a particular country or historical period. In our cosplay world, this definition encompasses much more.

The way to truly understand a costume is to break it down into categories, then into parts. Some categories of a costume include dresses/gowns, shirts/bodices/tops, coats, suits, undergarments, and pants/skirts. Then these categories can be further broken down into parts: A top can consist of sleeves, collars, yokes, and bodice pieces. Each part can be further broken down to include the details that truly make the costume, such as cuffs, pockets, and layers. If you really get excited about drafting your own patterns, further studying fashion terminology can help.

Taking Your Measurements

Before you take your measurements, there are a few things to consider.

You'll need to decide which undergarments you need for your particular cosplay. Are you going to wear a corset, just a bra, or maybe some shapewear? Or how about some foam muscles under a suit? Go ahead and gather the chosen undergarments and put them on to ready yourself for taking measurements. Tie a piece of ribbon around your natural waist to act as your midpoint. A lot of measurements are taken using your natural waist.

My two favorite measuring tapes; one 60″, the other 120″!

Be honest with yourself. Taking down your body measurements is sometimes like stepping on a scale. Not everyone likes it, and sometimes the results are not what we want, but it will be okay. You are choosing to create something for yourself, and you want it to fit you, right? You get to know your body very well during this stage of costume design.

When you are ready to take your measurements, I recommend grabbing a buddy and a measuring tape. Then stand up straight, look forward, breathe normally, and don't suck in your stomach.

LET'S MEASURE!

Even if you are only making a simple skirt, you need to take (and record) all your measurements because I guarantee you will refer to them over and over for different projects. For the sake of planning, let's take all the measurements that I think are needed the most in cosplay making. These are the basic measurements that everyone needs. Download the chart on the next page and fill in your measurements or record them in your sketchbook or journal so you can find them easily.

- Measure the circumference of your neck, shoulders, bust, wrist, waist, hips, thigh, knee, calf, and ankle.

- Measure your center front from the base of your neck down to your natural waist. Do the same for your center back.

- Measure from shoulder point to shoulder point on your front and back. To locate your shoulder

point, find the area on your shoulder where your shoulder starts to curve down toward your arm. Your shoulder point is the furthest spot before your shoulder curves down into your upper arm.

- Now let's move to the arms. Place the measuring tape at your shoulder point and measure the length of your arm down to your wrist with your arm straightened and then with it slightly bent.

- *Optional:* if your costume requires pants, measure your outseam and your inseam. Measure from your natural waist to your ankle to get your outseam and from your crotch to your ankle to find your inseam.

- *Optional:* depending on your intended hemline, you will also need to measure from your waist to your knee, your ankle, or the floor.

ACCESSING THE MEASUREMENT CHART ONLINE

To access the measurement chart through the QR code, open the camera app on your phone, aim the camera at the QR code, and click the link that pops up on the screen. Print and use the chart as many times as you need! For complete instructions, go to: tinyurl.com/11494-patterns-download

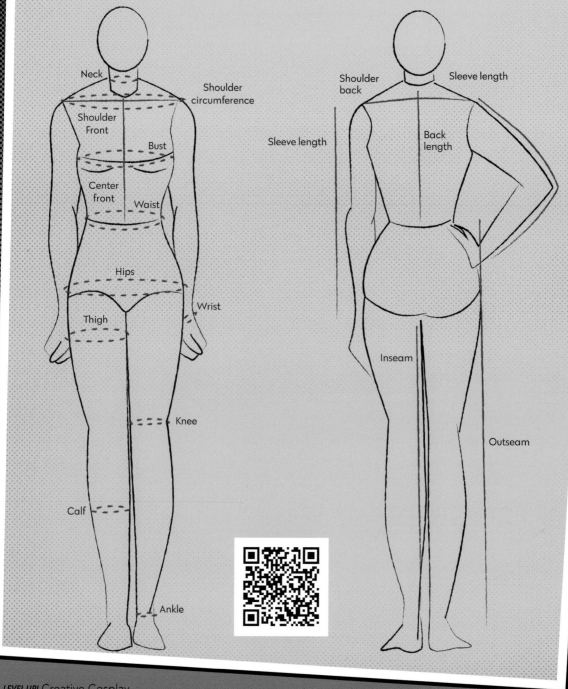

BODY MEASUREMENT SHEET

Neck

Shoulders (circumference)

Bust

Wrist

Waist

Hips

Thigh

Knee

Calf

Ankle

Center Front

Center Back

Shoulders Front

Shoulders Back

Arm (straight)

Arm (bent)

Outseam

Inseam

Hemline Measurement

Moving Your Measurements to a Dress Form

I think a dress form is necessary when you are creating (and draping) your own looks and patterns for cosplays.

Draping fabric on a dress form to create clothing is one of the oldest design methods, dating back to the eighteenth century. You can see your designs almost instantly come to life in front of you. Playing around with pinning, slicing, and making darts also helps you learn more about the process of making clothing.

There are a couple of types of dress forms from which to choose if you would like to get one. Keep in mind that you will probably need to pad your dress form to your measurements unless you have one custom made. Most are sold in standard sizes from 0 to 24. If you are purchasing a standard-size dress form, buy a size a bit smaller and pad it out, especially if your weight fluctuates.

My favorites are *professional dress forms*. They are solid, are often filled with material that can hold pins, and have no gaps. The ability to pin right into the form to hold the many layers of fabric you are working with is ideal! These dress forms are only available in standard sizes.

There are also *adjustable dress forms*. These are typically less expensive than the professional ones, but the biggest bonus is that they are adjustable to better match your measurements. With the turn of a dial, you can expand and contract the bust, waist, and hip measurements to fit you. These are a great starter dress form. The downside is that they are hollow, and you can't pin directly into them. The pins slide into the padding, so they are sometimes less secure. Plus, there are gaps in the sides of the form if you chose to expand it, creating areas where pinning to the form is impossible.

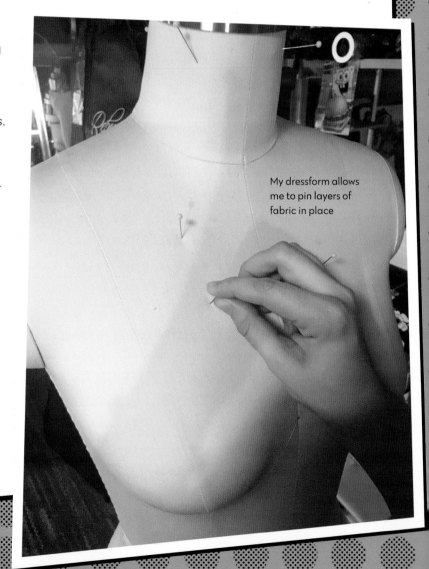

My dressform allows me to pin layers of fabric in place

PADDING OUT A DRESS FORM

If you have or choose to get a dress form, you probably need to pad it out to match your measurements.

To make sure your dress form accurately matches your body shape you will need padding materials. Some dress form manufacturers also sell padding in pieces or kits to be used with their dress forms. If shaped pieces of foam are available for your form, be sure to grab them! If these are not available I prefer to use *quilt batting* that I wrap around the dress form in specific areas until it mimics my measurements. You can also combine premade pads with quilt batting or other padding. Some people like to add an older bra or bra cups to get the correct cup size on the chest.

Use a measuring tape, your measurement sheet, and all the padding to pad the dress form as close to your shape as you can, pinning the padding in place as you go. Some people like to cover the padding with a super tight covering. This isn't necessary, but it does help keep everything in place. You can make your own covering or purchase one. Once you are satisfied with the shape, wrap the waist with a length of ribbon or twill tape to identify the natural waist.

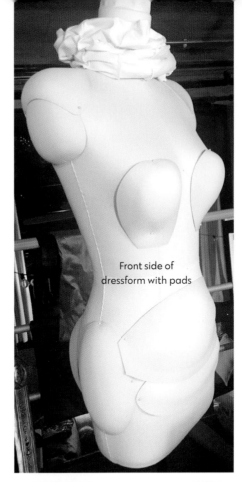

Front side of dressform with pads

Back side of dressform with pads

Front side of dressform with cover

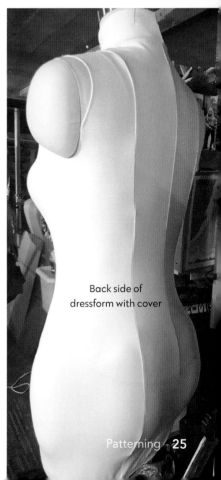

Back side of dressform with cover

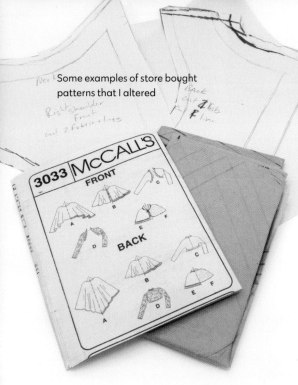

Some examples of store bought patterns that I altered

Draping Your Own Pattern or Using a Commercial Pattern

I know many of you are probably wondering, why drape? Why make your own patterns? So many patterns already exist in the commercial world. You are correct—they do. There are a lot of large and small pattern companies releasing tons of commercial patterns each year, and they are a great first step when you are starting to make cosplays. However, there are not always commercial patterns available for the look you want, or the patterns that exist do not get close enough to your actual measurements. Whichever is the case, when you are ready to design your own costumes, you'll want to know how to drape and draft your patterns (see From Drape to Draft, page 29).

It is not necessary to find a commercial pattern that exactly matches your vision for your cosplay. You can "Frankenstein" together multiple patterns or you can alter existing patterns (yours or commercial), which can save the cost of purchasing multiple patterns. For example, you can use the sleeve from one pattern and the bodice from another, lengthen a dress skirt to make a train, or add a peplum to the skirt or bodice!

Here are a few quick and easy ways to adapt patterns. Learning these simple tricks can help you save time, money, and stress if you choose to start with a commercial pattern.

ADD VOLUME

Use the *slash-and-spread method* to add volume to the pattern. For example, if you want more volume in the top of a sleeve near the shoulder, add perpendicular cuts in the paper pattern from the armhole edge toward the hem and fan out the pattern strips. Spread the pattern piece sections out until it is the necessary size. Tape the revised pattern piece onto a piece of blank pattern paper. Trace around the edges to create a new, larger pattern piece. You can use this method anywhere you want more volume.

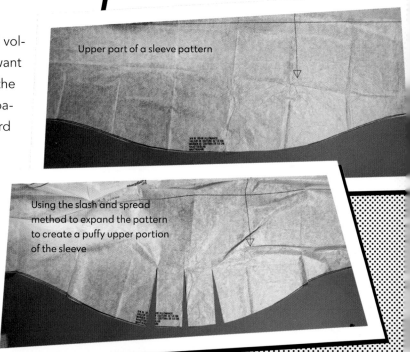

Upper part of a sleeve pattern

Using the slash and spread method to expand the pattern to create a puffy upper portion of the sleeve

REDUCE VOLUME FOR A MORE TAILORED LOOK

If you want a more tailored look, consider *overlapping* your pattern or *making a dart* to reduce the fabric volume.

Overlapping requires you to cut into your pattern, as with the slash-and-spread alteration method, but here you overlap the pieces to make the area smaller. You might have to slash and overlap several times so the pattern lays flat. Once you have overlapped the pattern sufficiently, tape it down, place a new piece of pattern paper underneath, and draw your new pattern piece.

Darts are used for taking in areas with extreme curves. They are often already drawn on a commercial pattern, but if not, it's easy to add them. Grab your pattern and pinch the area you want to take in, tapering the width of the pinch until it comes to a point (the endpoint of the dart). Pin the dart. You might want to hold the pattern up to your dress form to make sure the endpoint meets the end of the curved area of your body. Then mark the stitching lines that form the dart on both sides of the dart. Once you have the markings, you can remove the pins. This is now a transferrable mark that you will copy onto the fabric to show you where to stitch the dart(s).

Adding a dart into the pattern to help reduce the bulk around the waist

Darts in a skirt pattern

What the skirt pattern looks like when the darts are taken in and pinned

SHORTENING AND LENGTHENING

This is a simple adjustment, and most commercial patterns have a line indicating where to shorten and lengthen.

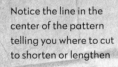

Notice the line in the center of the pattern telling you where to cut to shorten or lengthen

To *shorten a pattern*, fold along the lengthening/shortening line and overlap the pattern. Tape the overlap in place.

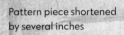

Pattern piece shortened by several inches

To *lengthen a pattern* cut along the lengthening/shortening line and spread the two pieces of the pattern apart the desired amount. Insert paper into the gap and tape the pieces together.

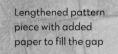

Lengthened pattern piece with added paper to fill the gap

FROM DRAPE TO DRAFT

Draping is the term used for placing, positioning, and pinning fabric to a dress form and is often the first step to creating your own patterns. Where and how you place the fabric is up to you, but it is quite freeing to let yourself be pretty organic at this stage. Draping is both easy and hard; you'll need practice to nail it down and understand it. I recommend reading about and watching (via YouTube) how designers drape all kinds of garments. With time and practice, you will probably never buy a commercial pattern again.

COSPLAYER: Jedimanda
COSTUME: Princess Anastasia from *Anastasia*
I bought a cage crinoline and skirt pattern and then draped the bodice, overskirt, and sleeves to create this costume

Permanent
maker

Tracing
wheel

Pencil

Muslin fabric

Tools of the Trade

To get started you will need a few standard items:

- Sharp fabric scissors, smaller scissors for trimming, a pencil, markers in multiple colors, a fabric tracing wheel and marking pens, straight pins, a tape measure, and, of course, your dress form.

- For draping fabric, I like to use muslin because it's a good medium-weight material that can mimic other fabrics. Muslin is a bleached or unbleached, lightweight cotton cloth with a plain weave. It is inexpensive and most sewists use it for draping. You might want to buy it in bulk if you plan to pursue pattern making or if you are draping a big outfit like a ball gown.

Muslin fabric

Close up ● ── ● Drape tape

Smaller
Gingher
scissors

Permanent
maker

Gingher scissors

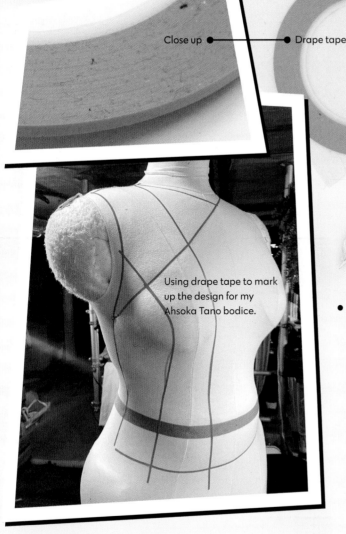

Using drape tape to mark up the design for my Ahsoka Tano bodice.

- One tool that I recently started using is drape tape, which is a narrow tape, usually ¼˝ or narrower, with an adhesive back. You use this tape to draw design lines out on the dress form. Then you take a length of muslin, place it over top of the tape, and trace the taped pattern onto the fabric. It's a great method for any garment that is form-fitting. It's also a great tool to use to mark off the bust, waist, hips, neck, and shoulder lines before draping your fabric.

Basic Draping Technique

Now it's time to drape. It's important that the straight grain of the muslin runs parallel to the vertical center of your dress form when you are draping pattern pieces. If you go off grain, the muslin could stretch and you might end up with a shape you don't want.

When you are draping the fabric on your form, just drape half! Unless your design calls for an asymmetrical pattern piece, draping only half of what you need saves time, muslin, and brainpower. Once you have the half pattern set (design lines drawn, darts pinned, fit perfected, waistline determined, etc.), you just trace half, flip the piece over and trace the other side for a full pattern piece.

If your garment has a unique design, it is better to drape the entire bodice or skirt, as I did for my Yennefer dress from *The Witcher* (see Patterning, page 19).

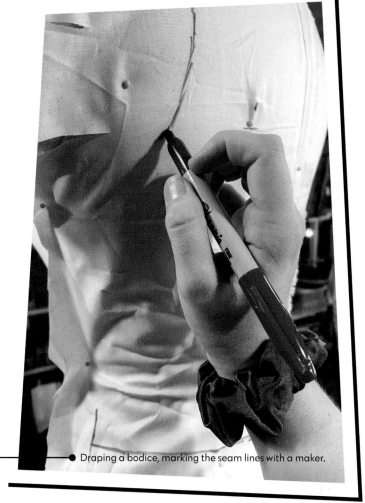

Draping a bodice, marking the seam lines with a maker.

1. Remember to put the necessary undergarments on the dress form before you start.

2. Keep your source material and sketchbook nearby.

3. I recommend draping each piece you need to make separately.

4. Pin the edge of a large piece of muslin across the front of the dress form, either from shoulder to shoulder of the torso for a bodice or a top, or from one side of the waist to the other for a skirt. Extend the fabric straight across the dress form to the side seam. Pin it in place along the side seam for the moment. **A**

TIP

Make sure the lengthwise grain of the fabric runs up and down the dress form.

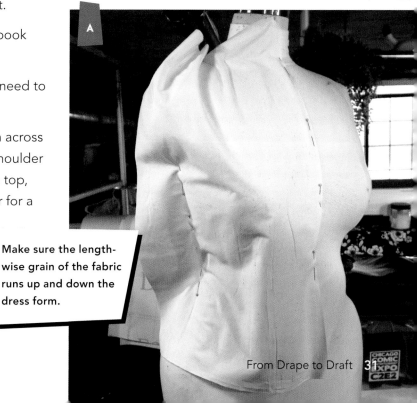

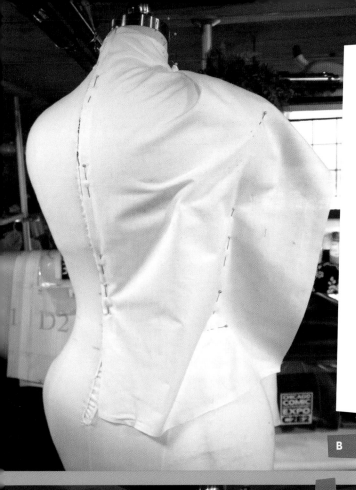

5. Pin the edge of the second large piece of muslin across the back of the dress form, either from shoulder to shoulder of the torso for a bodice or a top, or from one side of the waist to the other for a skirt. Extend the fabric straight across the dress form to the side seam to meet the front piece. **B**

6. Pin the two pieces together at the side, creating a temporary side seam. **C**

7. Establish your darts by pinning out the fabric. **D**

8. If there are sections of the fabric that are pulling because of the extra fabric, cut away the extra fabric and leave it on the ground.

B

C

D

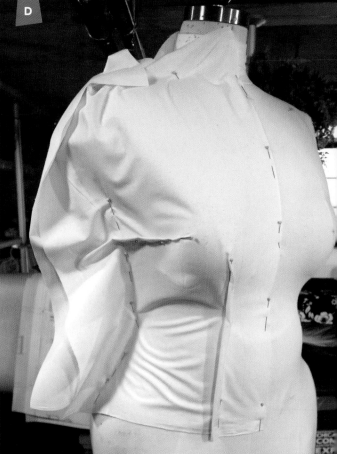

9. Once your fabric is on the form like a second skin (with no loose or pulling sections), draw your design lines. Start by drawing your neckline or waistline.

10. For sleeves or armhole finishes, I recommend marking about ½˝ away from the raw edge to indicate an armhole seam. **E**

11. Use a different color marker to draw seamlines. Make sure you know where you are connecting your pieces by marking notches along seamlines.

12. Once you have drawn all the seamlines and design lines on the muslin, label the pieces: front, back, side back, side front, or whatever designation will help you reassemble them later. **F**

13. Remove the pieces from the dress form, and you have just created your first draped piece! You'll use them to create the paper patterns. This may sound kind of crazy right now, but experimenting is key here. You will get the hang of it. Don't be afraid to do it again if you have to.

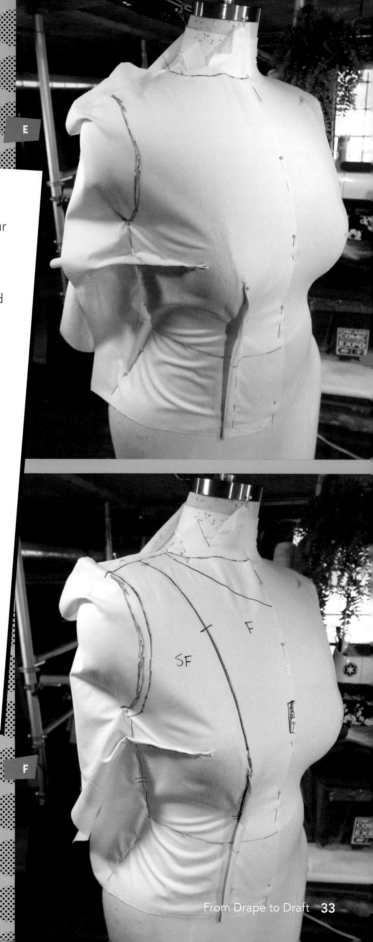

WHAT IS A SLOPER?

If you research draping and pattern making, you will come across the word *sloper*. A sloper is a block pattern that has been custom-fit to the wearer (or to the size being made). It's a standard-looking, flat pattern piece intended to be a base for whatever design style you want to create. If you get into doing a lot of custom pattern work for yourself, slopers are great to have. Making a sloper is very easy—it is a simple bodice or skirt with darts and no unique designs—and can save you draping time if you need to create multiple looks for one body size. Trace the sloper and add design lines to the copy. By adding and removing darts, tucks, pleats, folds, and any design lines and curves from your traced sloper, you achieve a new design each time.

From Muslin to Paper

Once the draped muslin pieces accurately represent your costume piece, you need to clean them up and use them to make the patterns. Take them off the dress form and press them if they are wrinkled.

Lay a large piece of newsprint or sewing pattern paper under the muslin pieces. Use fabric weights to keep the pieces in place. Run a tracing wheel around the edges and over all the design lines and seamlines to transfer (copy) them to the paper below. The pressure of the tracing wheel makes holes in the paper.

Remove the muslin piece from the paper and use a marker to draw in all the transferred lines, including matching notches. You will need to add the intended seam allowance, usually ½″, to every side to allow you the additional fabric needed to sew the pieces together.

Label all the pieces. Now you have a finished, fresh new pattern for your original design.

COSPLAYER: Jedimanda
COSTUME: Grogu from *The Mandalorian*
A great example of a
costume draped from scratch

FABRIC KNOWLEDGE

The variety of crazy designs that cosplayers can create sometimes requires a bit of a deeper dive into the fabric bin. Basic cotton, linen, satin, and spandex fabrics do not fulfill every idea we have for our cosplays. Sometimes we need to exit the garment fabric aisles and look elsewhere.

Indoor and outdoor upholstery fabrics that I've used in multiple cosplay projects

The Magic of Upholstery Fabric

Welcome to the upholstery fabric section! Upholstery fabrics have been my secret weapon for years. I've made everything from ball gowns to cloaks, and from corsets to jackets, all with materials found in the section favored by home decorators. Upholstery fabric is typically used for everything except garments and is meant to cover furniture and drape windows. A lot of upholstery fabric is created for outdoor use and can handle being out in the environment. These materials are usually heavy, but their weight can vary. Just take a stroll through the aisles, touch the various types of upholstery fabrics, and you can feel the difference.

Close-up of my Doctor Strange cape showing heavy-duty upholstery fabric paired with specialty trims and embroidery

COSPLAYER: Jedimanda
COSTUME: Nadja from *What We Do in The Shadows*

There are so many benefits to using upholstery fabric, including the variety of patterns, textures, and fabric weights and content you can choose from. And another benefit is the increased width. Most upholstery fabrics are 55″ wide or wider, which is perfect for ball gowns and long cloaks. Sometimes I need something regal for a ball gown, and many of the "bridal and costume" options in the regular fabric aisles just do not cut it because the fabric quality is sometimes not as high as home decor fabric.

If you choose to use upholstery fabric for your cosplay, there are a couple of things to know.

- You need to pay attention to the fiber content, especially if you are dyeing the fabric or planning to wash it. If your fabric has wool, silk, or a blend of those fibers, wash a sample first to make sure it's okay to manipulate in the washer. Wool and silk usually should only be spot cleaned, but hey, it's your fabric. Feel free to experiment!

- Most upholstery fabric is stiff and may be too stiff for cosplay wear. If you want it softer, you have to soften it with fabric softener! It's amazing how quickly your fabric will go from super stiff to a beautiful fabric you can make into a ball gown.

- I recommend overlocking or serging the edges before washing with softener and detergent to help prevent frayed edges.

While I worked on Anastasia, I kept in mind Russian court gowns, which often boasted rich patterns. I was lucky enough to find upholstery fabric that met my patterned vision.

Draping the train for my Anastasia gown.

COSPLAYER: Jedimanda
COSTUME: Ahsoka Tano from the Star Wars franchise
Heavier upholstery fabric was the right choice for this cloak. It offered the texture, weight, and the outdoor look I was envisioning.

UPHOLSTERY FABRIC DISADVANTAGES

Buying upholstery fabric does come with some disadvantages, one being the cost. You will quickly notice that the price of upholstery fabric is much higher than that of regular garment fabric. This is mostly because of the high cost of making this fabric, as well as the amount you get per yard. As I said earlier, the fabric width of upholstery is usually much greater than the standard garment fabric bolt. If you can, use coupons for this purchase! For example, I know Joann Fabric and Craft Stores often have big sales on upholstery fabrics, and you are also allowed to use the big percentage-off coupons for them. Quickly, your $40-per-yard fabric can become a $20-per-yard fabric with a coupon for 50 percent off. Stock up with those coupons and save!

Another way you can save on fabric cost is to thrift it! Check out thrift stores for upholstery fabric that is still on the furniture item or off it. You can find some treasures there if you are willing to carve up a piece of furniture or wash second-hand drapes over and over again.

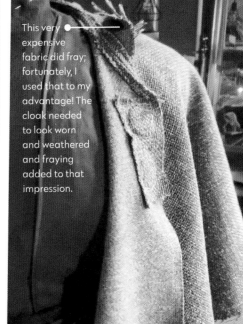

This very expensive fabric did fray; fortunately, I used that to my advantage! The cloak needed to look worn and weathered and fraying added to that impression.

Real or Faux: Leather and Fur

LEATHER

Leather is honestly one of my favorite materials to work with. It's versatile, durable, and doesn't fray! It takes dye and paint well, thus making the finished look of the cosplay very professional. But I also understand the downside of using real leather in my cosplays, including cost, environmental issues, and that it's a dead animal's skin! Thinking about that makes me cringe slightly. But I think if you understand the true craft of leatherwork and are willing to be sustainable about it, you can make leather work for you.

Close-up of the back of my Kitana full leather bodice

Work in progress: the front of my Kitana full leather bodice

COSPLAYER: Jedimanda
COSTUME: Kitana from *Mortal Kombat 11*
I chose real leather for the bodice of this costume. I was challenging myself by using leather for the first time and I found that I loved working with it!
Photo by World of Gwendana

What is leather? It is simply a material that is made from the skin of an animal. Leather has been used for over 1,000 years in garment making, tool creating, furniture building—you name it. A long time ago, people used the entire slaughtered animal for food, shelter, and clothing, the ultimate recycling program, I would say. As the world got smaller and societies developed, fashion trends became the only reason to kill certain animals. Not to get too graphic, but hunting animals just for fur and skin would dismantle animal populations. The fashion industry would use all the feathers, furs, and animal skins, leaving the animal population to become extinct or almost extinct. The history behind this topic is fascinating and sad. But I also understand the need to use animal skins and furs for utility. The animal is no longer with us, so let's use the animal parts and not let them go to waste, which is why when I feel leather is truly the right choice for a costume, I use leather from animals also used for food. It's a dicey conversation, but it's a necessary one, especially in the fashion world.

How Leather is Made

Let's talk about how leather is made and its uses. Leather goes through a process called tanning. The process involves altering the protein structure of the skin, making it durable, more flexible, and less susceptible to decomposition. During this process, leather is often dyed a myriad of colors.

The most common type of leather is cowhide: about 65 percent of all leather is from cows. Other animal skins that are turned into leather include pig, goat, sheep, alligator, snake, and zebra. There are more types of animal skins used for leather, but they are much less common than those listed. Different exotic leathers have their own distinct look, feel, and price point. You can purchase full hides at your local leather store. You can also purchase scraps for smaller projects, like belts and appliqués.

COSPLAYER: Jedimanda
COSTUME: Ahsoka Tano from the Star Wars franchise

Work in progress shot of Ahsoka Tano's belt. The base belt is made from vegetable-tanned leather.

Types of Leather

There are two different types of tanned leather: vegetable tanned (sometimes called veg-tan for short) or chrome tanned.

VEGETABLE-TANNED LEATHER is the technique that uses vegetables or tree bark to tan the leather instead of chemicals and minerals that can be harmful to the skin or the environment. This process often requires time and skill but results in a great product.

CHROME TANNING is the exact opposite of vegetable tanning. It uses chemicals and minerals to break down the skin proteins. The chrome salts are thrown in with the leather in giant drums and rotated to mix the two in a process called washing the leather. This lower-cost method is much faster than vegetable tanning, and the entire process can be completed in less than a day. The most commonly available leathers are chrome tanned. If you want to avoid this type of leather, make sure you read the labels and ask the leather professionals selling them to tell you which process was used.

Suede

Don't forget about suede! Suede is the underside of the animal skin, and it is also used in garment making. I've used it many times. It's thin, soft, and matte. Suede can add a fun textural change to your piece if you are using a lot of leather: just flip over the leather and use the suede side!

Recycled Leather

One of my best tips for cosplayers is to go hunting for recycled leathers. You often can find some amazing treasures in thrift stores, including real and expensive leathers at affordable prices. Look for older leather jackets from throwback fashion decades. Look at the belts and shoes to see if you can reuse and repurpose them. It's an environmentally safe way to be sustainable while also helping your wallet. Don't be afraid to spot clean or paint over problem areas. Experiment and go for it!

FAUX LEATHER

The opposite of real leather is fake, or faux, leather. Faux leather is a synthetic material made to look like leather by layering a base fabric with a plastic (polyurethane) coating. The plastic coating is colored and textured to look like leather.

● Work in progress: making Doctor Strange's armbands with faux leather strips for detail

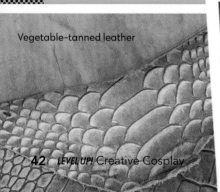

Vegetable-tanned leather

Suede

Synthetic leather

COSPLAYER: Jedimanda
COSTUME: Doctor Strange from
Marvel Cinematic Universe
Costume features faux leather
in the armband's trim details

TIP

If you plan to sew faux leathers, make sure to buy a nonstick or roller presser foot for your sewing machine (see Journey Through Presser Feet, page 76). These feet will help the material slide under the foot and needle, thus making your sewing experience so much better.

Doctor Strange's belt with some pieces of faux brown leather

Why Use Faux Leather

Why use faux leather instead of real leather? One simple reason is that it's not a dead animal's skin. Most of the time, it's cheaper as well. It's water-resistant like leather and comes in multiple colors and weights. However, faux leather also has an environmental impact. The production of the chemicals and plastics used in making this synthetic fabric require petroleum and huge amounts of energy, often relying on fossil fuels. These fabrics are not organic and do not break down in landfills. Just some food for thought.

Be cautious when you purchase faux leathers. Some can be more porous than you think, so they are less water resistant and can hold sweat within the fabric. They can have a plastic feel, get stuck under a sewing machine if you use the wrong presser foot, and can look cheap. However, if faux leather fits your budget, use it!

The more our fashion world discovers and experiments with sustainable fabrics, the more faux leathers I see on the market. Vegan leathers are taking the world by storm right now. These special materials are made using cork, pineapple leaves, mushrooms, and so much more. The process that creates them requires skilled craftsmanship, and they are expensive. I think the ingenuity here is marvelous, and I look forward to using them in my cosplays when the price comes down.

FUR

I only work with fake fur, but you can certainly choose to use real fur. For cosplay, fake fur is cheaper and easier to use. I'm not a fan of buying real fur unless it's a thrift find or a borrowed item, but there are options out there if you want more of a realistic look. A lot of faux fur fabrics today have great textures and colors available.

Faux fur

Work in progress: making my Daenerys Targaryen cosplay. To get the look I wanted I topstitched strips of red faux fur fabric onto white faux fur fabric and then trimmed the red for an integrated look.

Strips of faux fur and white synthetic leather, ready to stitch together to sew into my white faux fur coat for Daenerys Targaryen cosplay.

Working with Faux Fur

Using OLFA's ESK-1 Beginner Craft Knife to slice faux fur. This knife is great to use because it only exposes a small section of the knife and is ideal to just slice the fabric and not the pile.

Using hair shears to trim the coat's fur.

Here are a couple of tips when preparing and working with faux fur.

- Before you go shopping, determine what type of *pile* you want. Pile refers to the length of the fur hair. Some faux fur fabrics have a very short pile, and some have pile as long as 4″.

- Use a craft or art knife rather than scissors to cut faux fur. Scissors tend to cut the fur so that it looks uneven. Keep the pile together and slice the back of the fabric with a craft knife just enough to go through the fabric but not enough to go through the pile. If you don't exert too much pressure you won't have as much of a mess to clean up afterward.

- Faux furs can be dyed or airbrushed, and you can even use markers to change the color of the pile. Get experimental with faux furs, and don't let the fur mess stress you out!

- Sew faux fur with a standard zigzag foot and be sure to clean your machine frequently.

- To change or reduce the pile, use hair shears rather than sewing shears.

COSPLAYER: Jedimanda
COSTUME: Nadja from *What We Do in The Shadows*
I made Nadja's capelet with a faux fur featuring 3″ long pile

DYEING FABRIC

When I was shopping for fabric for my cosplay inspired by Sally from *The Nightmare Before Christmas*, I knew I needed a several different colors. Her iconic look is a patchwork dress made from several different colors of fabric. I had a strong feeling I was going to have to dye a few pieces to achieve the tones I needed. Some of the colors were similar in tone, so buying one fabric and dyeing a portion of that fabric another color gave me two different fabrics to work with. It saved me money, which I also love. Dyeing fabric is a terrifying adventure for a lot of cosplayers, so I'm telling you: Yes, it is terrifying, but it's not hard. Dyeing fabric is a process. With practice and patience, this is a great skill to have in cosplay creation. It can save you money and create a more custom look for your creations. With just a little practice and patience, you will be dyeing more fabric than you can imagine.

COSPLAYER: Jedimanda
COSTUME: Sally from *The Nightmare Before Christmas*

What Can Be Dyed and What Can't

Most fabric can be dyed. If it's porous or fibrous, it can be dyed. Different fibers in fabric take dye differently. Understanding what fibers your fabric is made of is the first big step in dyeing. Read the fabric bolt before purchasing, especially if you know you are going to dye the fabric. Natural fibers and synthetic fibers dye differently.

NATURAL FIBERS like linen, cotton, wool, and silk are the most popular; hemp, flax, and jute are a little less popular. Linen and cotton are easy to dye: you just need to dunk them in hot water with dye! Wool and silk, however, require a more involved process and are not often dyed for cosplay. Although natural fibers can take dye better and often turn out very vivid, not all cosplayers use natural fiber fabrics for their garments. We often use synthetic fabrics or polyester blends.

FEATURING SALEM, MY CAT, a top down view of my Sally cosplay from Nightmare Before Christmas

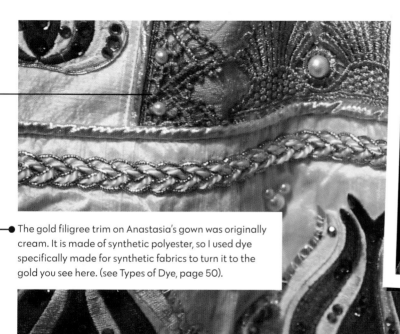

The gold filigree trim on Anastasia's gown was originally cream. It is made of synthetic polyester, so I used dye specifically made for synthetic fabrics to turn it to the gold you see here. (see Types of Dye, page 50).

COSPLAYER: Jedimanda
COSTUME: Princess Anastasia from *Anastasia*
Once dyed, the filigree trim on the bodice and skirt adds the regal touch I was looking for.

SYNTHETIC FIBERS used in cosplay are mostly polyester and polyester blends. These fibers require a special dye for synthetic fabrics. The resulting color isn't always true to the color on the box. It seems to depend on how hot the water is and the amount of fabric in the dye bath. I've dyed many synthetics in my cosplay career, and to be honest, the results weren't always ideal. I can't scream loudly enough to test your dye bath with a strip of fabric before you dye your full length of fabric. I call it a strip test, for lack of a better, less sexy word. Cut strips of your fabric about 2″ × 5″ and dip them into a test pot of dye made with boiling water (see How to Dye Fabrics, page 53). For each test, write down the amount of dye used and how long the strip was in the dye bath to pinpoint the exact formula you need to get the color you want. Synthetics are tricky to dye, but it is definitely possible.

Types of Dye

There are a lot of different types of dye. Just take a gander down that loud tie-dye aisle at your local craft shop. Sometimes I get overwhelmed by the options. So many colors, powders vs. liquid, cheap vs. expensive. So let's keep it simple.

NATURAL DYES are dyes derived from plants or organic minerals, which can include berries, roots, bark, leaves, and more. Many people use strong black tea or coffee grounds to change the tone of lighter fabric colors, usually to achieve an aged or weathered appearance.

SYNTHETIC FABRIC DYES are derived from chemicals. These dyes were created in a lab back in the nineteenth century. They were specifically made to dye clothing faster and cheaper during the industrial revolution. Many people wanted options in color, creating the push toward synthetic dyes. The color mauve was the first synthetic color, and it was created by mistake. In 1859, William Henry Perkin was a young chemist trying to create a treatment for malaria when he stumbled upon this pale purple color. The color became all the rage in fashion when Queen Victoria wore a dress dyed with Perkin's mauve to the Royal Exhibition of 1862.

A view of the large variety of Rit Dye available at any craft store.

LIQUID, POWDER, OR PACK?

DYE POWDERS come in many color options and are cheaper than liquid dyes, but they are only used for natural fiber fabrics. If you have even one ounce of polyester in your fabric, choose the liquid synthetic dyes.

LIQUID DYES are already diluted and ready to pour directly into the hot water bath. They are available for dyeing both natural and synthetic fibers.

DYE PACKS are easy to use because you just throw the whole pack into the bath. No measuring or timing is necessary, but you only get one shot at the dye bath. This means that the dye bath becomes diluted the more you dip the fabric in and out, especially with different fabric pieces. So if you want to keep the dye bath at its highest color strength, I recommend dyeing everything in one shot. This works for both synthetic and natural fibers.

Choose your dyes wisely! Be sure to select a dye that is specifically formatted to work on the fiber content of your fabric.

How to Dye Fabric

Before we get into the nitty-gritty of dyeing fabric, we need to talk about safety.

Anytime you are dyeing fabric, you should wear a respirator mask—unless you are using natural dyes like tea and coffee. When you are using synthetic fabric dyes, you must wear a mask. It may not seem like you need one, but mixing the dyes with hot water creates chemical fumes that you might breathe in. Be sure you have adequate ventilation when you dye! The respirator mask only protects you, not other people or pets in your home. Dyeing fabric often entails using tools and utensils commonly used in the kitchen. However, once used for dyeing, your pots, spoons, and the like should no longer be used for food preparation or serving. It is best to purchase pieces that you intend to only use for dyeing.

GATHER YOUR SUPPLIES

Start by making sure your dye area is clear of anything you do not want dye on. Splashes happen, and I have countless pieces of clothing with colorful dye splashes! You might also want to gather plenty of colored towels or towels you are not afraid to get dye spots all over.

Then you need to choose the right dye tub. If you are dyeing synthetic fabrics, you need boiling water to keep the synthetic fibers open to allow the dye to absorb into the fabric. To keep the water boiling, you need the dye tub to fit on the stovetop, which probably means you will use a large pot. The pot needs to be large enough to soak the fabric completely and be able to move it around to let the dye soak in. I dye natural fibers in boiling water too.

If you prefer not to use boiling water to dye natural fibers, you can use a 2–3 gallon bucket, large plastic bin, or even your washing machine. The dye packaging will indicate the water-to-dye ratio. Some dye instructions suggest that you weigh your fabric to see how much dye you need. Other dyes might provide a suggested amount of water, and all you need to do is dunk in the fabric and stir it around with a large utensil.

I recommend preparing a small dye bath first with a smaller ratio of dye to water. Cut swatches of your fabric and dye a sample to determine how much time you need to dunk your fabric to get your desired color.

You will also need: a large spoon to stir the fabric, large tongs to remove the fabric from the dye bath, an apron, disposable gloves, a hair tie to pull back long hair, and of course, the dye and the fabric.

A Scraps of fabric ready to test dye

B Fabric ready to dye! Make sure to use a spoon dedicated to dyeing and no longer for food use.

FABRIC DYEING STEPS

1. Assemble your fabrics. Many fabrics fray as soon as they hit the water, so save yourself a headache and finish the edges by overlocking, serging, or using pinking shears. Wet the fabric before dunking it into the bath. **A**

2. Create the dye bath and put the fabric in the water to soak. Dunk it periodically. Watch your time! **B**

C Removing the fabric from the dye pot.

TIP Dyeing fabric is a lot of trial and error! I dye in 30-second intervals, and if the fabric needs to be darker, it can go back in the bath.

3. When the fabric appears to be the right color, move the dye bath to a clean sink with cold running water. Remove the fabric from the dye with large tongs. Remember that the water will be very hot. **C**

4. Rinse your fabric in cold water until the water runs clear. Try to spread out the fabric as you move it under the cold water. **D**

5. Pat your fabric dry or put it in your clothes dryer. Finally, I recommend washing the fabric with a mild detergent and hanging it to dry. **E**

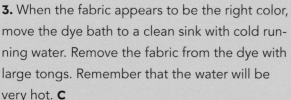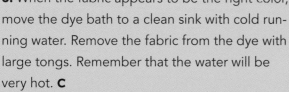
D Rinsing the freshly-dyed fabric in cold water.

E Gently pat your dyed fabric dry!

SALT?

Salt in a dye bath helps the fibers absorb the dye. Most commercially available dyes already have salt added. Read and follow the manufacturer's instructions on the dye box to see if added salt is necessary.

COSPLAYER: Jedimanda
COSTUME: Sally from *The Nightmare Before Christmas*
Sally was the perfect dye project because her colors are not perfect. I was able to use dyeing to achieve different tones of the same fabric so they worked well together. Because her dress is meant to look imperfect, I didn't have to be overly precise in my dyeing.

PAINTING FABRIC

Choosing and Prepping Your Fabrics

I must admit, I prefer painting fabric over dyeing! Most folks don't know that I have a college degree in fine art painting. I think a true art piece can be made by adding hand-painting details onto your cosplay or garment. However, anyone can paint fabric—no degree in fine art is necessary!

You can paint on any fabric. You just need to know how porous it is first.

IF YOUR FABRIC IS HEAVY OR THICK, such as denim, twill, or canvas, you might be able to paint on it directly without a prepped surface.

IF YOUR FABRIC IS SHEER OR THIN and you can see a weave such as organza, chiffon, or gauze, you need to take extra precautions in preparing your fabric. Prep the surface with gesso or several layers of Mod Podge decoupage medium so the paint won't seep through the fabric.

FOR FABRICS LIKE LEATHER OR VINYL, you don't necessarily need to prep the surface, but you do need a certain paint additive (see Mediums, page 57).

You need to prep either fabric or paint to prevent your paint application from bleeding through, cracking, or peeling off. I can't imagine spending all the time working on something beautiful and having it fall off your fabric.

THE FIRST STEP IS TO PREWASH YOUR FABRIC (if the fabric can be washed). Do not use fabric softener. Be sure to look up the fiber content to make sure the fabric is washable (silks and wools often are not machine washable). The prewash removes chemicals and stiffeners and preshrinks the fabric. Once your fabric is prewashed, let it hang to dry, and get your painting tools ready.

My Scarlet Witch cosplay fabric; the fabric on the right was a great pattern but it was a bit too pink. I painted the fabric to subtly change the color to a more burgundy color.

Painting Supplies

You will need paints, fabric mediums to blend with the paint, and brushes and sponges (or an airbrush if you have one).

PAINT

How to choose your paint? Well, it's ultimately about what you want your design to look like. About 90 percent of the time, I use acrylic paints combined with a fabric medium. Acrylics are the most common paint to use for fabric painting. However, you can use inks, watercolors, and of course, the classic: puff paint! The paint aisles at craft stores have so many options. Brands like Jacquard, Angelus, Golden, and Liquitex give you the highest pigment concentration

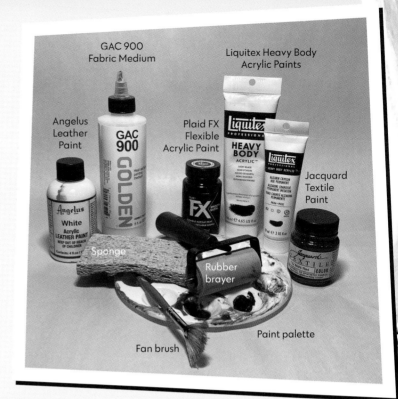

GAC 900 Fabric Medium

Liquitex Heavy Body Acrylic Paints

Angelus Leather Paint

Plaid FX Flexible Acrylic Paint

Jacquard Textile Paint

Sponge

Rubber brayer

Paint palette

Fan brush

and are sometimes premixed with fabric medium and ready to paint directly onto the fabric. Pre-mixed paints tend to cost more, and while the cheaper brands may seem more wallet friendly, the paint might be thinned out so much that you need to add multiple layers to achieve the color you want. If you are painting a large area, you might want to consider thinning a higher quality paint and using a larger brush. Higher quality paints generally contain more pigment, so fewer coats are necessary. Experiment with all the brands to see what you like best.

When you are buying paint, keep the total area to be painted in mind to try to determine how much paint you'll need. If I had a dime for every time I didn't buy enough paint—let's just say I'd be buying more expensive fabrics for my cosplays!

PLAID Leather Studio paints

PLAID FX Flexible Acrylic Paints

Angelus Leather Paints

COSPLAYER: Jedimanda
COSTUME: Captain Marvel from Marvel Cinematic Universe
After watching *Captain Marvel* and seeing other variations of her suit, I opted to paint my costume to give it a new look. I used Angelus paint to repaint my Captain Marvel cosplay.

FABRIC MEDIUMS

Fabric medium is blended into paint so that the paint will adhere to fabric and be flexible once painted. It is an absolute must unless you are using paint specifically formulated for fabric. Since you will be wearing the hand-painted piece, the fabric will be moving and possibly exposed to the elements and fabric medium prevents your paint from cracking or peeling.

GAC 900 Fabric Medium

Angelus Leather Paint

PLAID Fabric Medium

Fabric medium can be thick or thin; the thinner mediums are usually used for airbrushing. It looks white but dries colorless, so do not worry about the medium changing the color of the paint. However, the medium might dilute your paint to the point of lowering its opacity, so more than one coat might be necessary.

Medium is usually added to the paint at a one-to-one ratio. I suggest combining your paint and mediums in a separate container or palette rather than on the main palette you are using. Once mixed, just start painting. You will see that the medium helps the paint go on more smoothly and evenly. You can use any brush for application. The mediums I use require heat setting after application. Check the manufacturer's instructions on your chosen medium to ensure that your paint sets properly. To heat set your fabric, cover your piece with a pressing cloth and press it with an iron or heat press for the length of time indicated on the package. This will help the paint set and be ready to take on the elements.

Using a combination of GAC 900 Fabric Medium and Liquitex Heavy Body Acrylic in alizarin crimson to paint my textured fabric for my Scarlet Witch costume

BRUSHES OR SPONGES

There are a variety of paint application tools—choose the one that works best for you and your desired result. A sponge works if you want texture, but most of the time a simple paintbrush will do. I highly suggest watercolor or acrylic paintbrushes. Oil paint brushes are a bit too stiff for fabric paint application. Buying a pack of inexpensive brushes is great, but the cheaper the brush, the more the bristles will fall out. It's the worst feeling to have to peel paint off to remove a trapped bristle. Don't forget to take care of your brushes after you are finished painting. Clean your brushes thoroughly with soap and water and then lay them out to dry, or your brushes will be ruined.

COSPLAYER: Jedimanda
COSTUME: Nadja from *What We Do in the Shadows*
Don't limit your painting to fabric! I used very small brushes to paint the tiny bats onto the trim buttons.

A *soft rubber brayer*, typically used for printmaking, works great on textured fabric.

Air compressor hose

Air compressor

Airbrush cleaner

Golden High Flow Acrylic Paint

Airbrush cleaner tools

My airbrush

Createx Airbrush Colors matte top coat paint

Airbrushing

Airbrushing is the perfect way to paint a large area that needs to be covered with paint when you just do not want to be stuck with a lot of brushing. It is also great when you want to have a small gradient color shift without dyeing your fabric.

COSPLAYER: Jedimanda
COSTUME: Kitana from *Mortal Kombat 11*
To match the blue color in my all-leather bodice
I had to paint fabric for my pants. I used Angelus
Leather Paint paired with Angelus 2-Thin in my
airbrush to match the colors.

An airbrush is a great tool to have in your cosplay toolbox. I was very intimidated by airbrushes before I bought one and tried it out. I was taught traditional painting with a good old brush and paint. Having to get a consistency of paint, medium (if needed), and air pressure was tough at first, but after some practice I was so comfortable with it that I truly love airbrushing now. It's such a fun and fast way to lay down paint. You can build up layers with multiple passes with the airbrush.

An airbrush is basically an air-operated tool that sprays paint. If you are new to airbrushing, I would start by purchasing an airbrush kit, which should include everything you need except the paint and a mask. Most kits include the airbrush, an air hose, an air compressor, and cleaning tools. You can always add, remove, or upgrade different tools as you develop skills. The packaging instructions will include the information you need to know to keep the compressor well pressurized. You won't have to mess with the compressor too much; you quickly will find the optimal pressure that you want for your spray.

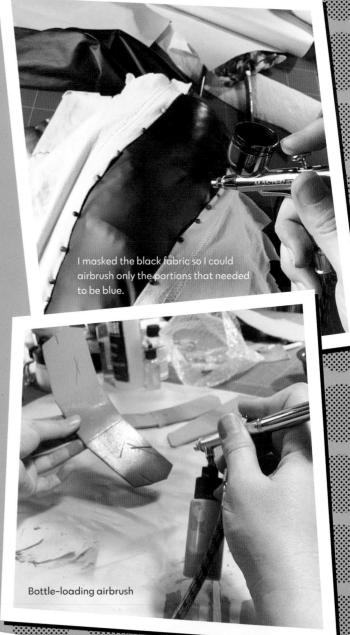

I masked the black fabric so I could airbrush only the portions that needed to be blue.

Bottle-loading airbrush

SELECTING AN AIRBRUSH

There are top-loading and bottle-loaded airbrushes. Either one works for fabric painting. The top loaders are good for mixing paints within the brush but you have to completely clean out your airbrush every time you change colors. Bottle-loading brushes are often more expensive, but I like them because I like to mix my paints ahead of time and have them in separate bottles ready to spray. If you opt for a bottle-loading airbrush, buy lots of bottles so you do not have to continually empty and clean out bottles.

GETTING STARTED

Practice, practice, practice. This is a technique that requires practice to get comfortable with the airbrush.

1. *It's very important to work in a well-ventilated area.*

2. Keep paper handy to practice the application and assess the color.

3. Once your paint is loaded, turn on the compressor, put your mask on, and give it a go. Holding the airbrush like a pencil, push the trigger down for air and pull the trigger back for paint.

- With the trigger depressed, push the trigger fully forward to get a narrow stream of paint, which is ideal for painting thin lines and small details.

- Once your paint it flowing, pull the trigger back to widen the spray, and pull all the way back to get a wide spray area, perfect for painting larger areas and for laying paint down faster.

- Getting closer to your surface and pulling farther away also gives you different results. Practice a combination of these approaches to conquer the airbrush and transform your cosplay.

TIP

Watch for splatter! If your paint is coming out of the airbrush and splattering over your surface, you probably have a clog. Check your manual and unclog the nozzle before painting further.

FINISHING

Okay! Your airbrush painting is finished! At this point, you need to heat set the paint. Consult the manufacturer's instructions on the paint and fabric medium you used (see Fabric Mediums, page 57).

You also need to clean out your airbrush. Remove the excess paint and fill your airbrush or bottle attachment with the cleaner. Turn on the compressor and run the cleaner until it runs clear. Double-check in and around the nozzle to see if there are any paint clogs, and set your airbrush aside to dry.

COSPLAYER: Jedimanda
COSTUME: Kitana from *Mortal Kombat 11*
Once painted, the pants and armbands now tonally match the bodice and the costume works as a whole.

CREATIVE FABRIC
STABILIZING

Sometimes you are going to need a firm structure with–
in or under your fabric to achieve the design you want.
It could be for a superhero suit where you need fabric-covered foam
armor, or it could be for a cloak that needs a standing collar. Getting creative with fabric stabilizer is really fun and provides another opportunity
for creativity. Move beyond the traditional stabilizers, and consider fabric
manipulation sewing techniques, foams, and thermoplastics.

Fabric Manipulation Sewing Techniques

In *Creative Cosplay* I share how to use commercially-available stabilizers, but these do not always result in the look you need for your
costume. Fabric manipulation is a fun way to experiment with fabric
and expand your sewing skills both on a machine and by hand. There
are so many different sewing techniques that you can use to add
some fun details and structure to your piece. Let's go over a few.

COSPLAYER: Jedimanda
COSTUME: Lydia Deetz from the cartoon *Beetlejuice*

GATHERING

Gathering is a common sewing technique that reduces the width of a piece of fabric and provides texture. Gathering to establish structure requires a lot of fabric—almost twice what you would normally use. To create structure (rather than fullness), you need to run multiple rows of basting stitches side by side on your piece to build the framework of structure that you need. Hold the thread tails and gently pull the fabric along the basting stitches towards the center of the fabric to create the structured piece. Experiment to get the look you want!

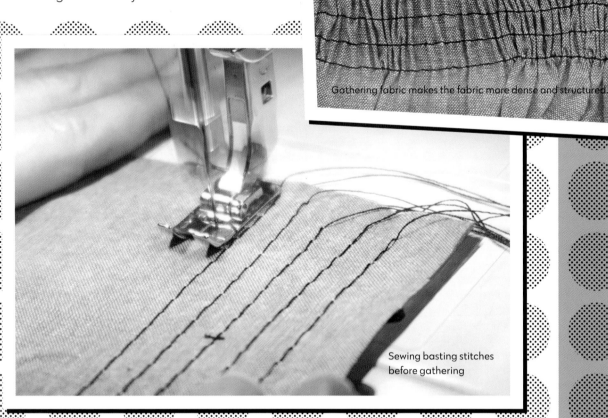

Gathering fabric makes the fabric more dense and structured.

Sewing basting stitches before gathering

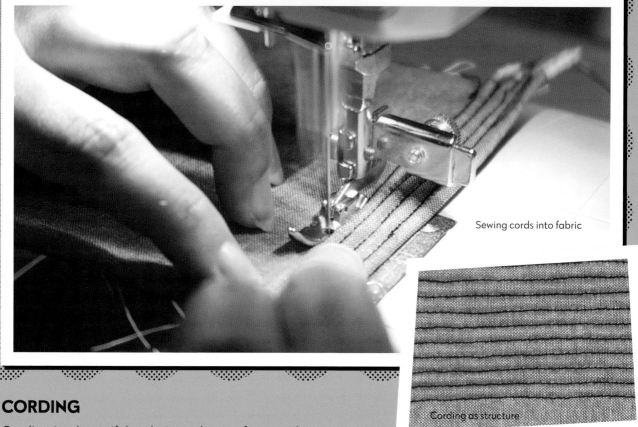

Sewing cords into fabric

Cording as structure

CORDING

Cording is a beautiful technique that is often used in corsetry and gown making. Sewing channels around lengths of cord raises your fabric and adds subtle texture, particularly when the channels are sewn close together.

Cording is added between two layers of fabric.

1. Stitch from edge to edge across the top of the piece.

2. Slide a length of cord between the layers as close to the first row of stitching as possible.

3. Use a zipper foot on your sewing machine and stitch another row of stitching parallel along the bottom of the cord and as close as possible to the cord (see Journey Through Presser Feet, page 76).

4. Continue adding lengths of cording as desired.

This technique requires some intense precision between you and your machine (or hand) when you stitch. Work carefully and slowly to keep everything lined up properly as you stitch. Encasing the cording adds stiffness to your piece, with a very neat final texture and look.

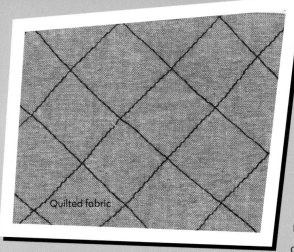
Quilted fabric

QUILTING

Quilting can be utilitarian, creative, or both. It can add bulk and structure to your fabric pieces. The art of quilting is vast, and I don't intend to go into great detail about it, but I want to show you that even though quilting is traditionally a home decor art form, many designers and cosplayers use quilting techniques in garments. In traditional quilt making, a layer of *batting* (any soft insulating material) is sandwiched between two layers of fabric and all three layers are stitched together. For cosplay, your choice of batting will be determined by the needs of your costume piece. If you are trying for a puffy look, select a thicker, fluffier batting, if you need structure, use a stiffer material as your middle layer. I recommend a thinner batting if you want to use quilting as a garment detailing technique and don't want to overheat your body. I suggest you experiment and stitch a few samples with different battings.

1. Gather two layers of fabric and a layer of batting

2. Create a quilt sandwich by layering the batting between the two fabric layers. Pin or baste the layers together so they do not shift when sewn. Stitch lots of fun stitches in rows or in a creative organic design. It's all up to you. You will instantly see a structure start to form the more quilting you add. Plan out your design and have fun with those stitches.

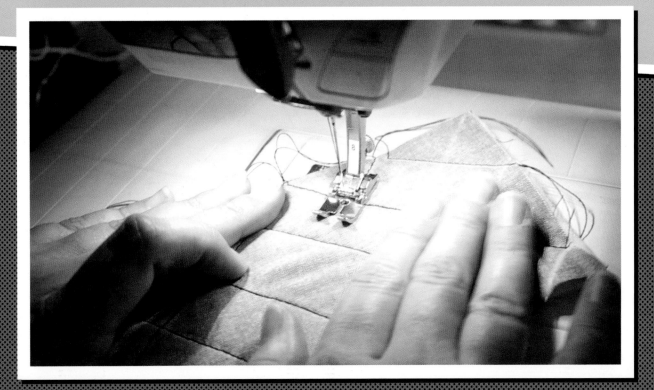

I used parallel quilted lines to stabilize Qi'ra's shoulder area and provide visual interest.

COSPLAYER: Jedimanda
COSTUME: Qi'ra from *Solo: A Star Wars Story*
The quilting in the shoulder section of the collar added both the structure I needed and also a subtle texture shift that accentuated the rounding of the shoulders so the look didn't end up boxy.

Foams

Foam is a rather new material for sewists to use as a stabilizer, but it is cheap, and it works great. In addition to being thicker than most stabilizers, when stitched the lines are really visible. Where bold lines are needed, foam is a great choice to add the needed depth to the fabric. Foam is also ideal for adding structure. The best part is that it is sold in a lot of different thicknesses.

COSTUME: Captain Marvel from the Marvel Cinematic Universe
Foam offered the clean, crisp lines and dimension I wanted in my Captain Marvel cosplay.

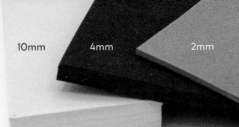

10mm   4mm   2mm

EVA FOAM

EVA foam, or ethylene-vinyl acetate foam, is a popular craft material for cosplay making. This material is commonly used to make armor or props and is sometimes used in garments as a layer under fabric. EVA foam comes in many different thicknesses, from 2mm to 10mm. Its durability and cheaper price point have made it a favorite among cosplayers. I love using EVA foam in multiple ways, but lately I've been using it underneath my fabrics to give a solid, smooth, and structured look. I've used it in my Captain Marvel and Kitana cosplays because they required an armored look and the depth of stitching in the foam gives the appearance of assembled pieces rather than sewn pieces.

This technique is simple: just stitch the garment fabric right on top of the foam. However, I do have some tips to share before you get started.

- I recommend using **BASTING SPRAY** to help keep your fabric adhered to your foam during sewing. Basting spray is a light glue that is used to temporarily hold two pieces of fabric or material together. It prevents the foam and fabric from shifting under the presser foot of your machine.

- I also recommend using **A WALKING OR NONSTICK PRESSER FOOT** to help keep the foam and fabric aligned while sewing (see Journey Through Presser Feet, page 76).

I used EVA foam to create the structure for my Captain Marvel armor.

Pieces of fusible foam stabilizer   Pieces of Fosshape

FUSIBLE FOAM

Fusible foam is more like interfacing than a stabilizer since a stabilizer is properly defined as a product placed between two layers of fabric. Fusible foam is made up of one layer of squishy open cell foam under a layer of tricot fabric with fusible adhesive. Sewable and stiff, this foam is a great material to have in your arsenal. I love using foam for collars, cuffs, and even breastplates. Follow the manufacturer's instructions to fuse the foam to your fabric and then the material is perfect to slip under your sewing machine and sew freely, since it does not gum up the needle.

1. You need a lot of heat and pressure to adhere the foam to your fabric. Each product works a bit differently so be sure to always read and follow the manufacturer's instructions. For some reason, this material can be tricky to adhere, so crank up your iron, grab a pressing cloth, and push heat directly onto the fabric (no steam) with the fusible foam underneath for about fifteen seconds.

2. After fifteen seconds, remove your pressing cloth and let the piece completely cool before moving it or checking to see if it has adhered. If it didn't adhere, press again for double the amount of time. The trick is to let it cool completely.

Now you are ready to go and use this material in your cosplays!

I used fusible foam stabilizer for most of the detail on Captain Marvel.

Fusible foam helped me stabilize this detailed piece for my Doctor Strange cloak.

COSPLAYER: Jedimanda
COSTUME: Captain Marvel from
Marvel Cinematic Universe

Thermoplastics

Thermoplastics are fairly new products, but they do exist! *Thermoplastic* is an umbrella term for a type of plastic that molds when heat is added via a heat gun or a steamer (depending on the brand). The packaging instructions indicate which heat source to use.

Thermoplastic brands such as Worbla, Wonderflex World, and CosplayFlex offer versions for almost every cosplay need. Often sold in sheet for direct use, there are also options available that are completely sewable. When you have a piece that you really need to retain its shape or to be rigid, thermoplastics are the right choice. Often, the sewable options are made of mesh that is very flexible even when cooled into shape. There are a few sewable options on the market including:

- **KOBRACAST** A thin mesh thermoplastic from Worbla which is stretchy when heated, tear resistant, and is sticky on both sides, allowing it to adhere to anything.

- **FOSSHAPE** This material was originally used in theater costume shops, and Wonderflex World has brought it to the cosplay community's attention. This material looks and feels like felt but is laced with heatable fibers. It's often seen as a buckram replacement, especially in hat making, so this thermoplastic is fun to use in accessory making. Keep in mind that there are several different weights of this material if you intend to use it for your cosplay. I would experiment with a sample piece before adhering it to your fabric. This is a fun, light, and versatile material to help give any piece in your cosplay the proper amount of structure.

Each product is used a bit differently and new products emerge frequently. Always read and follow the manufacturer's instructions to get the best results.

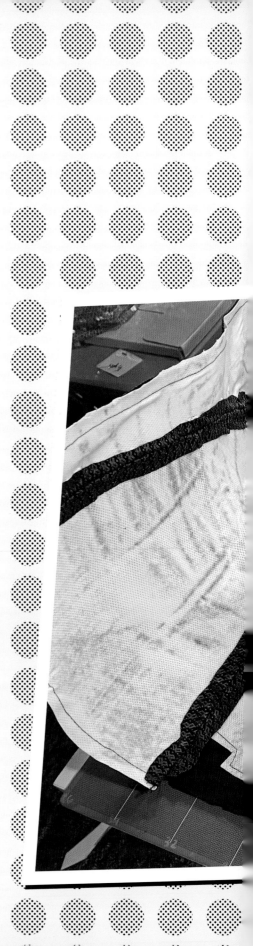

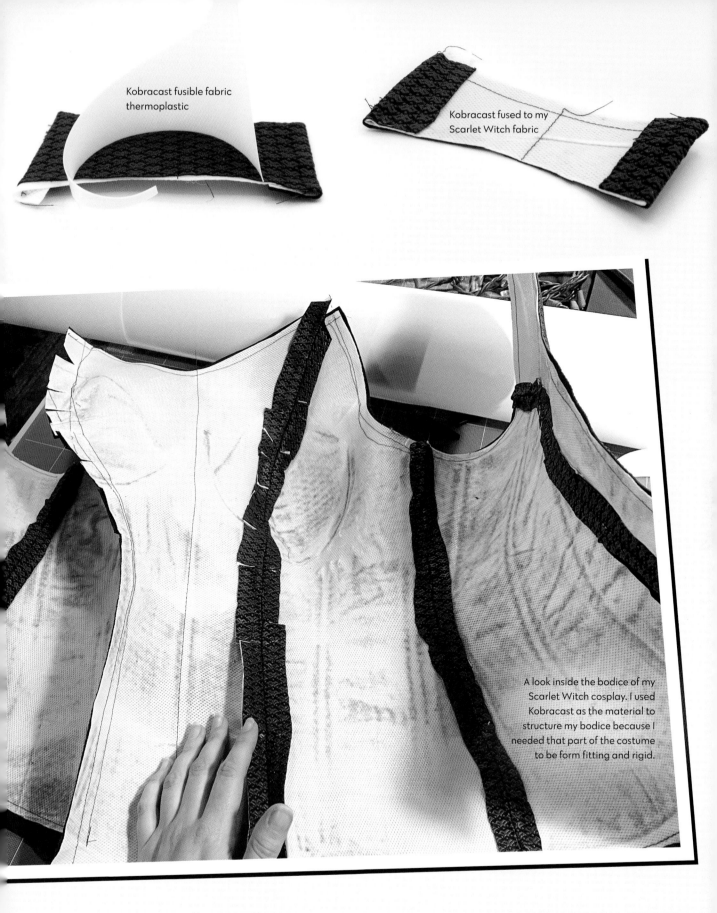

Kobracast fusible fabric thermoplastic

Kobracast fused to my Scarlet Witch fabric

A look inside the bodice of my Scarlet Witch cosplay. I used Kobracast as the material to structure my bodice because I needed that part of the costume to be form fitting and rigid.

SEWING MACHINE FEET, SERGERS, AND EMBROIDERY MACHINES

When I wrote my first book, *Creative Cosplay*, I didn't think I could have more to say to cosplayers about sewing. Turns out, I do! I want to cover more about sewing machine feet, sergers, and embroidery machines. Using these tools is a good way to level up your cosplay sewing journey, so let's dig in.

COSPLAYER: Jedimanda
COSTUME: Doctor Strange from Marvel Cinematic Universe
Photo by World of Gwendana

COSPLAYER: Jedimanda
CHARACTER: Wednesday Addams
from *The Addams Family*
Because I chose quilting cotton
for this costume, I used a serger to
finish my seams so that I
didn't have to deal
with the fabric fraying.

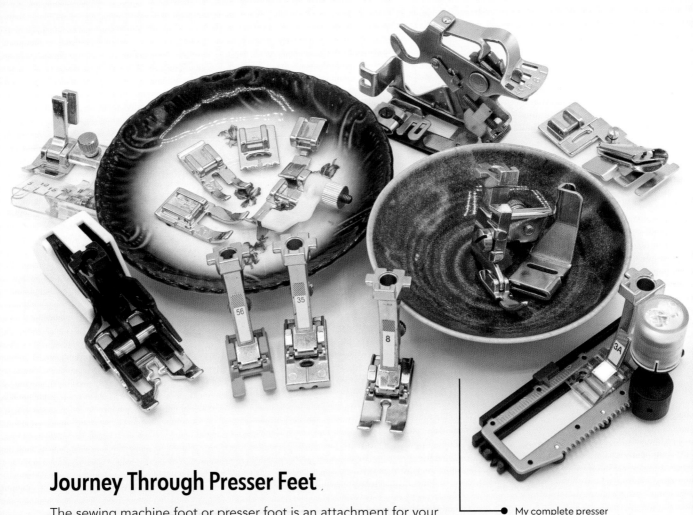

My complete presser foot collection

Journey Through Presser Feet

The sewing machine foot or presser foot is an attachment for your sewing machine that helps keep the fabric flat as it's fed through the machine by feed dogs that push the fabric from underneath. Up until now you have likely been using the standard or zigzag foot that came with your machine. However, there are so many different presser feet available—designed to help you sew different tasks!

The sewing machine foot is broken down into two parts: the shank and the foot itself. Each sewing machine manufacturer has a presser foot shank that matches their machine. In addition, some presser feet are sold as part of the shank and some snap on to the bottom of the shank. To be sure you are getting the foot you need and one that will work with your machine, always confirm that the foot you purchase is compatible with both the make and model (and sometimes even model year) of your machine.

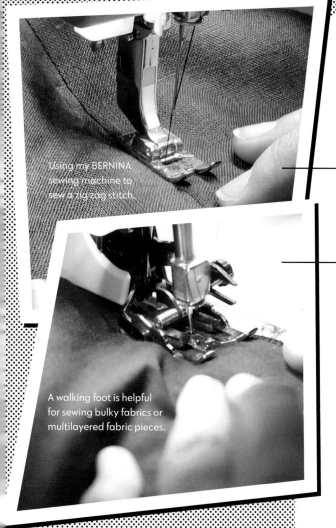

Using my BERNINA sewing machine to sew a zig zag stitch.

A walking foot is helpful for sewing bulky fabrics or multilayered fabric pieces.

TYPES AND USES FOR PRESSER FEET

General Sewing

For general sewing, use:

- **STANDARD OR ZIGZAG FOOT** Suitable for general sewing and some decorative stitches, this will likely be the foot you use the most and the one you are already comfortable using.

- **WALKING FOOT** A walking foot, sometimes called a dual feed foot or even feed foot, has a mechanism that helps the fabric move under the presser foot in tandem with the feed dogs. This foot is very helpful when you are quilting straight lines or sewing together multiple layers, bulky fabrics, or fabrics with pile, such as faux fur.

- **ROLLER FOOT** As the name implies, there are rollers on the front and back of this foot that help feed the fabric under your needle without bunching or snagging when sewing leathers, velvets, or other fabrics with uneven levels, nap, loops, or pile.

- **NONSTICK OR TEFLON FOOT** The slick coating on the bottom of the foot allows leather, faux leather, vinyl, plastics, and any fabric that can stick under a standard presser foot to glide under the foot without damage or tears.

Specialty Sewing

For specific sewing tasks, use:

Using my adjustable zipper foot to sew cording into fabric.

- **BUTTONHOLE FOOT** Most machines come with a buttonhole foot, but they can vary considerably from machine to machine, so consult your manual for information on how to use the buttonhole foot.

- **ZIPPER FOOT** Most machines are sold with a zipper foot and I can't recommend these enough—I love them. They are essential for installing a zipper and include the traditional, adjustable, and invisible zipper feet. Zipper feet have gaps on either side of the foot that allow you to sew close to the teeth of the zipper and the invisible zipper foot has a groove in the center that accommodates the zipper teeth so you can sew as close as possible to the zipper. Zipper feet can also be used when applying any trim that has a tape and are also helpful when enclosing cording.

- **HEMMING FEET** Specialty hemming feet are ideal if you hem a lot of gowns, skirts, sleeves, or pants. They save you so much time in extra steps. These feet automatically turn the fabric under while you sew. They include the blind stitch foot, edge stitch foot, zigzag hemmer, and straight stitch hemmer. Each of these feet and feet from different manufacturers can work a bit differently, so consult your manufacturer's instructions to learn how to feed the hem into the foot properly.

- **DECORATIVE SEWING** There are so many decorative sewing techniques and invariably each has a foot specially designed to do that task. You can do many decorative tasks with the basic feet listed above, but if you have a technique in mind, there is likely a foot available to do it. For example, if you plan to do a lot of appliqué, look to see if your machine is compatible with an appliqué foot.

Many of you are probably asking if you need all these feet to sew cosplay things. The answer is no. I started sewing with about 3 different feet, the traditional zigzag foot, a zipper foot, and a buttonhole slider foot. I then grew my collection over time with the needs of my cosplays. I will honestly say I use the same five feet for most of my cosplay making. My recommendation is to slowly move out of your comfort zone. Grab one of the feet that came with your machine, but that you do not already know how to use. Read up and learn how to use that foot. You'll really start to see how specialty feet can help you save time and headache on tasks that you do frequently.

My new favorite nonstick foot!

TOP COSPLAY SEWING MACHINE FEET

• Traditional zigzag foot

• Zipper foot

• Invisible zipper foot

• Walking foot

• Nonstick foot

My serger! Bernina Bernette 203 Overlock Machine, 3 thread model

Sergers

Was there a time when you cut a fabric and it immediately frayed? Was there a time when you were stitching a seam on stretchy fabric and the threads just snapped? Let me introduce you to a machine that can help you with those issues: the serger! A serger, also known as an overlock machine, stitches a seam, trims the excess from the edge of the fabric, and overcasts the edge of the fabric as it feeds through the machine–all in one step! It is a wonderful machine. I've been using one since I started sewing, and it is invaluable. It's main benefit is that it can save a considerable amount of time and can help your garment last longer.

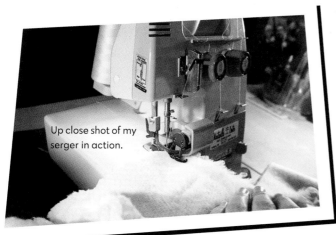
Up close shot of my serger in action.

A serger may not be an absolute must for beginner cosplayers, but it is a machine that I highly recommend if you do a lot of sewing for your cosplay. It is perfect for short deadlines! You have a choice to trim or not to trim the fabric edge as you pass it under the machine's foot. This machine is great for seaming together very stretchy pieces. I once used just this machine to make an entire bodysuit.

There are all types of sergers. The most basic and inexpensive models stitch with three different threads that work together to create the overlock stitch. The width of the stitch is usually narrower than it is for four- and five-thread sergers, but this serger can still sew a rolled hem if you can move or cover the trimming blade (see the serger's user manual).

Four-thread sergers can perform more stitch functions than three-thread sergers, and they are more expensive. If you want a wider stitch selection, consider buying a four-thread machine. Five-thread machines are the most expensive, but they offer more choices in stitch type. They usually include options for chain and cover stitches, which are used in the ready-to-wear garment-making industry. For cosplay, I recommend a three-thread machine because sometimes simpler is better—plus it's the type I've been using for years.

TIP Sergers cannot replace sewing machines, but standard sewing machines can do an overlock stitch. The stitch itself takes a while to do on a sewing machine but you can do it. Sergers are much more efficient, but it does require some practice to get used to the speed!

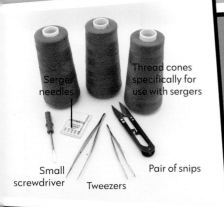

Serger needles

Thread cones specifically for use with sergers

Small screwdriver

Tweezers

Pair of snips

USING A SERGER

Learning how to use a serger is extremely easy once the machine is threaded. Grab your fabric, slide it under the machine's foot, and lower the presser foot. Once the fabric is placed, just hit the pedal to activate the machine, and you are off! No pushing or pulling your fabric—the feed dogs do all the work. Just watch your fingers and the fabric. Now that you know how to work the machine and are comfortable with it, let's go over the most complicated part about using a serger: threading it.

Not all projects require the same thread color, so you need to know how to rethread the machine and change the thread color. I remember that the first time I threaded my serger, it took me a few nights to get it right. But it turned out that I was skipping a whole step—as my machine manual clearly explained. Each machine is different, but while threading sergers looks complicated, it's not that hard to do. The machines have color-coded thread paths that help you thread the machine. The thread paths usually start at the back near the thread cones and move the threads through the tension dials and into the machine's mechanics. I recommend having a pair of long tweezers to help feed the thread through. Keep your instruction manual handy, and note that there is usually a mandatory order to the threading.

I know that the tension dials look tempting, but I recommend not messing with them too much. The tension dials feed the threads through the machine into a seam. If you increase the tension (turning the dial to the higher numbers), less thread will progress into the seam, and vice versa for the lower numbers. You can loosen the tension dials when you are working with thicker fabric if it requires a longer or narrower stitch. Again, the instruction manual will be helpful when you need to make machine adjustments.

AN EASY WAY TO CHANGE THE THREAD COLOR

Most sergers come threaded, so you might never need to thread it from the beginning. When it is time to change the thread colors, save yourself some time and frustration. Knot your new color of thread to the thread already in the machine and simply pull the new color through. Raise the needle so it is as high as possible, lift the presser foot, and turn the machine off. Tweezers help you hold thread ends.

1. Cut the threads close to the cone base, then remove the cones and put the new color thread cones on the cone holders. **A**

2. Keep the threads in the loops, and knot the ends of the threads together. Keep the knot small and strong. **B**

3. Pull the thread through for the needle first. Gently pull the thread through the serger up to the eye of the needle. Cut off the old thread and knot and then thread the new thread through the needle eye (tweezers can sometimes help with this step). **C**

4. Collect all the remaining threads and pull them through the serger at the same time. All the threads should pull through evenly; if it feels difficult or stuck, stop and look for a problem thread. Once all the new threads are through, lower the presser foot, press on the pedal, and run a stitch. The machine should automatically create an overlock stitch, and you are set to go! **D**

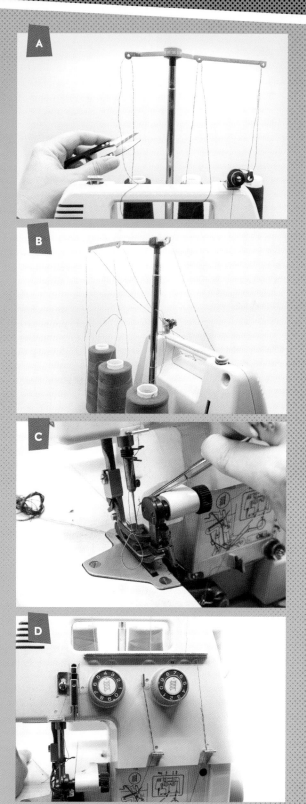

DO I NEED A SERGER FOR COSPLAY?

Do you need a serger for cosplay making? No, but it is absolutely a great tool to help you on your sewing adventures, especially if you work with a lot of stretchy fabrics. I also love that my serger can stop my fabrics from fraying like crazy. Finishing the raw edges of your seams with an overlock stitch makes your garment look just as lovely on the inside as it is on the outside!

Embroidery Machines

Embroidery is a hot topic right now! It involves a wide range of skills that you can learn to do both by hand and with a machine. Hand embroidery is fun, but it can be slow and take forever to complete. Cosplayers are often on a deadline, so let's kick it up a notch by diving into the world of machine embroidery.

Embroidery machines are computerized sewing machines that allow you to choose any design created in the file format that matches your machine and embroider directly onto any fabric. These machines already have designs set within the computer including various shapes, styles, borders, and patterns, and some machines also include copyright-free images. In addition to shaped designs, most embroidery machines have a set of fonts to choose from to create words.

Why have an embroidery machine? The biggest reason is that it's fast and hands-free! You can program a design into your machine, set the fabric in the hoop, press start, and let it go. Sitting and watching a machine do the work for you is so satisfying.

TIP There is an evolution going on right now, where companies are blending the typical sewing machine and the embroidery machine. Some of these combination machines offer embroidery stitch options that you can use to level up your detailing. Some machines have full embroidery options and some, like mine, allow you to do embroidery-type stitches in a line. Using a wide-eyed zigzag foot, you can select tons of different stitches that allow you to topstitch embroidery stitches just like you would a regular stitch.

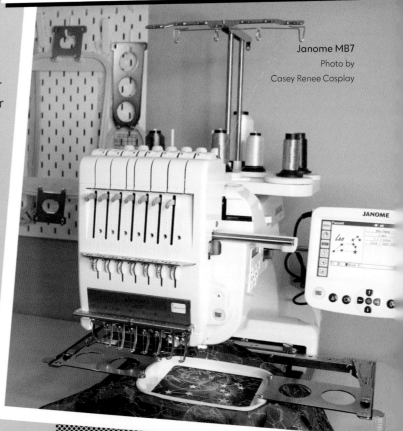

Janome MB7
Photo by
Casey Renee Cosplay

COSPLAYER: Jedimanda
COSTUME: Doctor Strange from
Marvel Cinematic Universe

An embroidery machine comes with bobbins, various tools, hoops in several sizes, and some allow you to purchase design software to create your own custom embroidery designs. Embroidery machines use a hoop frame system. If you are familiar with embroidery, you understand the need to stretch fabric over a hoop to keep it taut enough to stitch on. Once your fabric hoop is ready to go, hook it into your machine, choose your design, thread the machine, press go, and you are off to the races. Step back and enjoy watching the machine do all the work.

EMBROIDERY THREAD can be made of polyester, rayon, cotton, and silk. If you are planning to use an embroidery machine, make sure you are using the correct thread, or the machine might not function correctly (see your owner's manual). Embroidery thread is often thinner than regular thread and is sometimes metallic, sparkly, or even translucent. Usually sold on a spool, embroidery thread can be found next to regular sewing machine thread in stores. Just be sure to read the label!

TIPS

There are a couple of things to be aware of before the embroidery begins.

1. Always use interfacing so the embroidery doesn't pucker. Choose between fusible or non-fusible, water-soluble, or non-removable. There are so many interfacings out there for many projects; experiment and find the ones that work for you.

2. Check on the thread occasionally. When the thread runs out or needs to be changed, the machine will stop and wait for you to change it.

Stabilizers used in embroidery, both fusible and non fusible

CUSTOM EMBROIDERY DESIGNS WITH SVG FILES

Including custom embroidery in your cosplays can add a cool touch that people will instantly ask about. It might seem tricky at first, but the results are well worth the effort.

If you are interested in creating customized designs for your embroidery, you will work with SVG (scalable vector graphic) files to convert designs into a file format that your embroidery machine can read. Every embroidery machine has its own format, for example JEF for Janome or HUS for Husqvarna machines. When you buy an embroidery machine, the seller most likely will offer design software with the machine. This is the software needed to create designs and convert files for use on that machine. Having design software isn't necessary, but if you think you are likely to try custom embroidery design, you will need it. The software can be expensive and requires an up-to-date computer to run the software.

SVG files allow you or another person to create a graphic of any kind and export it to any embroidery design software to be converted to the machine's specific file format. An SVG will also allow you to scale the design larger or smaller without losing any detail. It will not become pixilated or blurry, which can happen with other file formats.

There are myriad graphics available for purchase. When you purchase premade graphics, you will receive an SVG file, and then the ball is in your court to convert it to your machine's special file format.

Learning how to navigate and use design software can be taxing and frustrating, but there are tons of embroidery experts out there who offer help digitally and in person. I highly suggest you seek them out. I love researching YouTube for help with this, as I still struggle with machine embroidery.

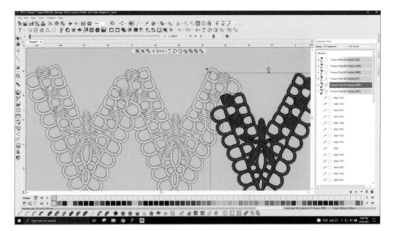

My friend Casey Renee Cosplay knew exactly the lace she wanted for her cosplay gown. She opted to create and execute the design with her embroidery machine so she got exactly the look she envisioned.

Before stitching, Casey was able to check the size and shape of her new digital design by comparing with her inspiration.

Photos by Casey Renee Cosplay

DIGITAL CUTTERS IN COSPLAY

Digital cutters have become very popular recently within the craft community. These machines can die-cut certain materials on a mass scale.

COSPLAYER: Jedimanda
COSTUME: Evie and Book of the Dead from *The Mummy*

My Cricut Maker die cutter

What is a Digital Cutter?

Digital cutters are taking the craft space by storm, and many cosplayers have one. But why get a digital cutter? Why can't you just use a craft knife and a self-healing cutting mat? Well, you can, but just like with the embroidery machine, having a machine do the work for you is so nice!

Whereas the embroidery machine stitches custom embroidery artwork for you, digital cutters slice and dice various craft materials for your cosplay needs. Trust me—these are handy!

A digital cutting machine is a machine that can die-cut certain materials using a variety of cutting tools, such as knives, razors, rotary cutters, and more. This machine was created for the home crafter to cut complex designs out of chosen craft materials quickly and easily. An additional advantage for cosplay is the ability to cut complex shapes in mass quantity. A costume often has repeated shapes or motifs and having a way to keep them identical and save time is amazing.

I wanted the beetle designs on my Book of the Dead to be identical, digital cutting was the best choice

The most popular brands are Cricut, Brother, and Silhouette, but more are available all the time. Each brand offers a variety of models. Choose a model based on the type of crafts you plan to make.

Craft Materials Suitable for Die Cutting

Die cutters can cut lots and lots of materials.
For cosplay it is fantastic at cutting:

- **CARDBOARD** is a particular favorite template material of mine. Use a normal to heavy-duty mat.

- **FABRICS OF ALL SORTS** are easy to cut using the rotary cutter knife. There is a mat specifically for fabric; just watch for fraying ends of the cut fabric pieces.

- **LEATHER** often requires finely detailed and small cuts, so using a cutting machine can help with this task. Use a heavy-duty mat for this one.

- **EVA FOAM IN DIFFERENT THICKNESSES** is the number one material I use with a cutting machine. I recommend the knife blade and a heavy-duty mat. Tape down the corners before cutting.

- **THERMOPLASTICS** might require multiple runs through the machine to cut thoroughly, especially if you are cutting fine details. Use a heavy-duty mat and tape down the edges.

- **STICKER PAPER/ADHESIVE-BACKED VINYL** is perfect for custom designs. Create a design and print it on this paper, then use your cutting machine to help trim around the shape. Use a lightweight to standard-weight mat.

Adding vinyls cut with my Cricut machine to my Queen Amidala skirt.

- **HEAT TRANSFER VINYL (HTV),** like EVA foam, is one of my favorite materials to use on my cosplays. Create any shape and cut it with the digital cutter—if your design is asymmetrical in any way or contains any text, make sure the mirror option is selected so the final result shows the correct shape! Then use heat to press the design onto your cosplay. Easy!

COSPLAYER: Jedimanda
COSTUME: Queen Amidala from the Star Wars franchise Digital cutting and heat transfer vinyl were the best choices when it came to the detail at the bottom of this gown. The design is so complex and I was on a deadline. Using SVG files ensured that I could make the motif larger and smaller as the design required and the digital cutter ensured that they were perfectly consistent.

My Cricut Maker die cutting machine open and ready to cut my next design.

Digital Cutting Software

Digital cutters are powered by software. Each model has a design program that you must understand to operate the machine and cut your designs. As with the embroidery machine, learning to use this software takes a bit of study and experimentation. Essentially, you upload a graphic file, arrange the material to be cut on a craft mat, and then tell the machine where and how to cut. Keep in mind that this is a cutter, not a printer; however, some machines allow you to use markers to draw designs on your material!

Most brands offer free web-based software to access and create designs for use with your cutter, but you may need to create an account to access it.

Before purchasing a machine, do some research to be sure the cutter you are interested in can handle the types of files you will want to cut. Read online reviews of the various software platforms to be sure they are compatible with your computer and your work needs.

SVG FILES FOR DIGITAL CUTTERS

If you need an image that you can't design or that someone else has already designed, you can purchase SVG files from other artists. The universal SVG format allows the software program in your cutter to read the file, create an outline of the design, and make it available for you to scale up or down. Then, you can cut the design with your digital cutter to your specifications.

Tools for the Digital Cutter

Every digital cutter uses tools to cut the chosen material. I like to break down these tools into *machine tools* and *handheld tools*. The information that follows describes the tools that I use with my Cricut cutter, but other machines have very similar tools.

MACHINE TOOLS

CUTTING TOOLS are used within the machine itself. The chosen cutting tool is placed in what is often called a *tool port*, which must hold a cutting tool to cut out your design. The tool port can hold a variety of blades, each meant to cut a different material or cut in a different way. Consult your machine's manual to select the correct cutting tool for the job at hand. I most often use a fine-point blade, knife blade, engraving tip, rotary blade, deep-point blade, or scoring wheel for my costume work, but there are others you can purchase.

Deep point blade

Rotary blade

Knife blade

Point blade

Cricut Maker blades

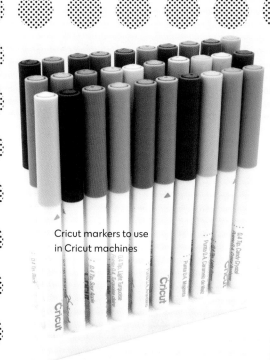

Cricut markers to use in Cricut machines

CRICUT CUTTERS WITH MARKERS

Some machines have a port for pens and markers, so you can use them to write and draw text, illustrations, pattern outlines, and certain images. There's even a fabric pen for marking fabric cuts. There are several different types of pen tip widths. Within the design software, you can see the fonts, shapes, and other options you can use with the pens and markers. Once you have your design, font, or shape ready in your program, just load the marker or pen into the port, lock it in, and go! This is handy for adding details that can't be cut.

MATS are important machine tools that are required for almost every digital cutter, and you'll likely need lots of them. They are the most important tool besides the machine. Your material sits on a mat while it is cut. The mats come in different grip strengths with different levels of adhesive; lighter grip strength for lightweight materials, and stronger grip strength for heavy and/or bulky materials.

TIP If the material doesn't completely adhere to the mat, try taping down the edges so the material slides smoothly under the blades.

I keep a variety of mats on hand, ready for use with all kinds of materials. For cosplay, I recommend the stronger grip mats because they hold thicker materials better than the other mats, which are more suitable for lighter materials like paper and fabric. Match your mat to your project before you begin cutting!

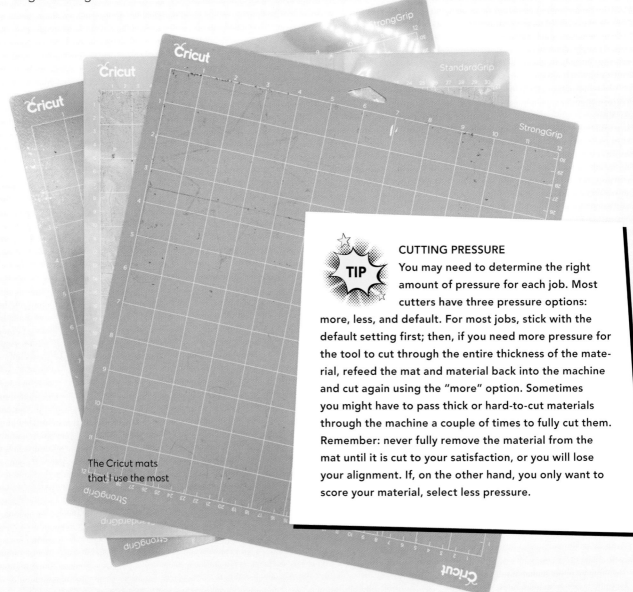

The Cricut mats that I use the most

TIP

CUTTING PRESSURE
You may need to determine the right amount of pressure for each job. Most cutters have three pressure options: more, less, and default. For most jobs, stick with the default setting first; then, if you need more pressure for the tool to cut through the entire thickness of the material, refeed the mat and material back into the machine and cut again using the "more" option. Sometimes you might have to pass thick or hard-to-cut materials through the machine a couple of times to fully cut them. Remember: never fully remove the material from the mat until it is cut to your satisfaction, or you will lose your alignment. If, on the other hand, you only want to score your material, select less pressure.

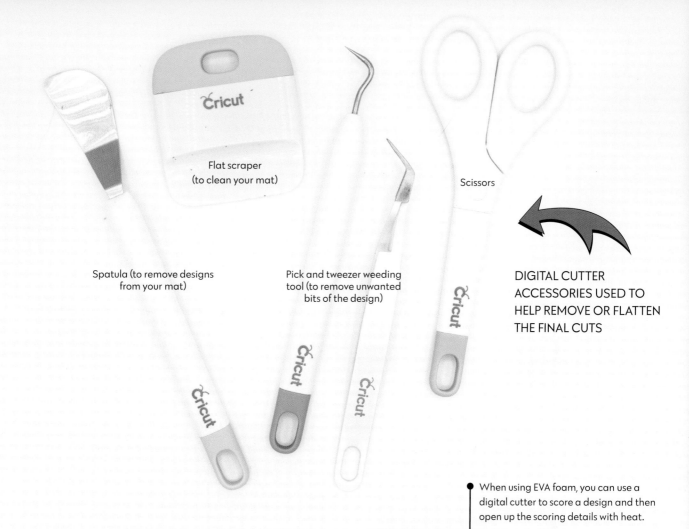

Flat scraper
(to clean your mat)

Spatula (to remove designs
from your mat)

Pick and tweezer weeding
tool (to remove unwanted
bits of the design)

Scissors

DIGITAL CUTTER
ACCESSORIES USED TO
HELP REMOVE OR FLATTEN
THE FINAL CUTS

When using EVA foam, you can use a digital cutter to score a design and then open up the scoring details with heat.

HANDHELD TOOLS

There is an assortment of tools that you need to apply your material to the mat and then to remove (or excavate) your designs from the mat. Scissors, scrapers, and tweezers usually are sold with the machine, but you can purchase extra tools. Use the tweezers and the scrapers to help remove the little and big bits that you don't need. Just be careful and know exactly what to pull off and discard before you dive in to remove everything from the mat.

Transfer tape for vinyl designs is useful to have on hand. Transfer tape allows you to lift, move, and apply designs while retaining the original spacing. Masking and painters tape also useful to have on hand to keep your materials on the mat during cutting.

Why Do I Need a Digital Cutter for Cosplay?

My favorite question is: Why? Why do I need this for cosplay?

I use a digital cutter to cut so many corners in limited crafting time. This machine helps me plan out tricky areas and acts as a second hand when cutting specific details or when cutting foam pieces in bulk. Its precision is undoubted. I can't get over the accuracy sometimes. For example, when I created my Book of the Dead cosplay from the film *The Mummy*, I needed specific hieroglyphs to stand out but not be cut out. I needed to score them on a piece of EVA foam so I could add heat and make them pop. Because these details were so small, I highly doubted that I could create them by hand. It worked out so well that my Book of the Dead is so accurate that it sometimes freaks me out! All thanks to my digital cutting machine.

Completed Book of the Dead before painting. The die cutter allowed me to add precise details to elevate this from an accessory to a movie–worthy prop.

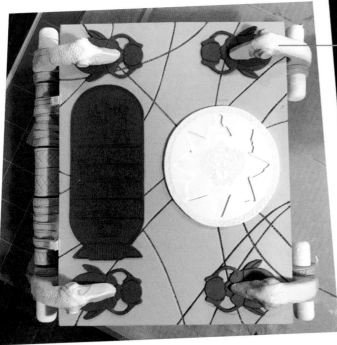

COSPLAYER: Jedimanda
CHARACTER: Evie from *The Mummy*

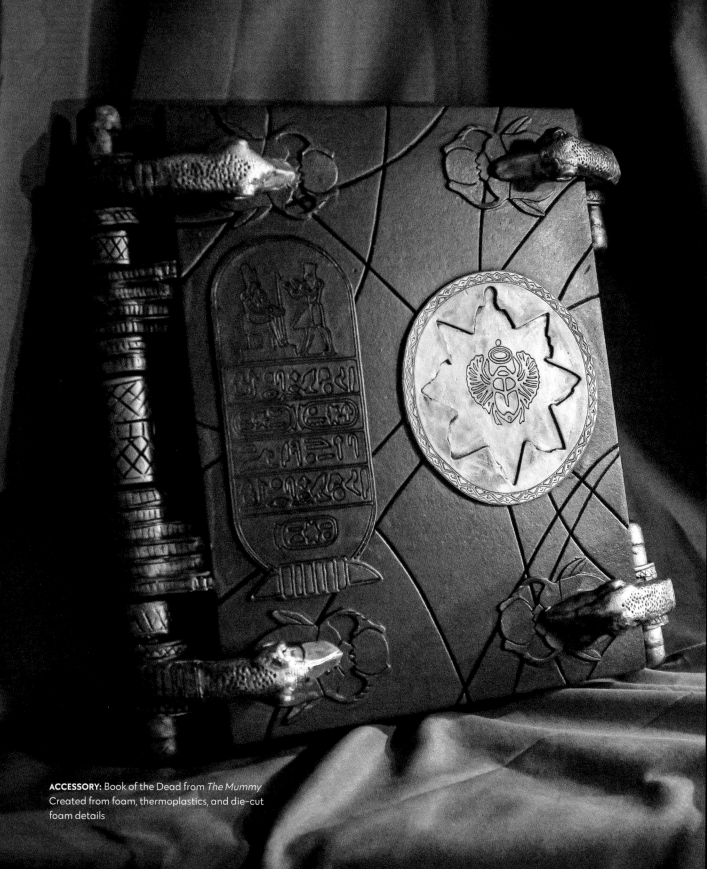

ACCESSORY: Book of the Dead from *The Mummy*
Created from foam, thermoplastics, and die-cut
foam details

BASIC LEDS AND LIGHTING UP YOUR COSPLAYS

Lights can be the biggest wow factor in your cosplay. Showing up to the convention floor with a glowing outfit or twirling on the convention competition stage wearing a twinkling crown will undoubtedly draw attention—in a good way! Adding LEDs to your cosplay is a newer technique that people are really diving into. It can be intimidating at first because it requires math, soldering, expensive tools, and lots and lots of batteries, but it's a great way to add originality to an existing design or take your original design to the next level.

When I was developing my Anastasia cosplay design, I knew I wanted my version of the crown to twinkle. Anastasia wears a special sparkling crown that is encrusted with animated diamonds, and I wanted to bring that sparkle to life in my cosplay. I thought a lot about how I was going to do it, whether I would install custom LEDs with a programmed computer board or develop a well-planned pre-strung fairy light layout with a battery pack hidden somewhere in the crown. I went with the latter, and I'm so glad I did. Planning and having choices for lighting up your cosplay is key. Practice experimenting with premade lights, and then work your way to custom circuitry. It's all part of the journey.

My Anastasia crown lit and unlit.

COSPLAYER: Jedimanda
COSTUME: Princess Anastasia from *Anastasia*

Adding lights to this helmet allowed me to achieve a higher level of screen accuracy for my Captain Marvel helmet!

COSPLAYER: Jedimanda
COSTUME: Captain Marvel from the Marvel Cinematic Universe

What Are LEDs?

LEDs are tiny light-emitting diodes. They are small and powerful in their light emission, and they have a longer life than non-LED lights. They are cheap and easy to find at many locations, and, more importantly, they emit no heat. I was always worried about that until I started creating circuits with them, but there's no heat! They come as single LED bulbs or as prestrung lights.

My Ahsoka Tano gauntlets with the green LEDs illuminated.

SINGLE LEDS

Single LEDs come in almost any color, and it's good to have a variety on hand. I usually purchase the variety packs from Amazon and store them in separate but connected containers.

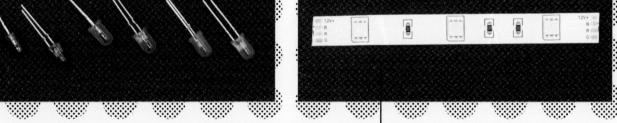

LED STRIPS

An LED strip is a flexible circuit board with small LEDs placed throughout and with an adhesive backing. They are water-resistant, coated for protection, and can be programmed to be multicolored and even animated! The strips emit a lot of light and are super bright. They do require a programmable circuit board to command the strip and tell it what to do. Each manufacturer's boards have their own programming needs and specifications. It would be impossible to cover all of those here, so when you select a board, know that you will need to learn how to program that specific board. This section will walk you through how to add simple LED lights.

Battery Power

LED work requires battery power, and there are two battery power options: primary and secondary. Primary battery types are designed to be discarded and cannot be recharged. They are the familiar coin cell, AAA, AA, and nine-volt batteries. The secondary type of battery is rechargeable and usually purchased as a solid unit. Rechargeable battery packs are often used for larger power needs such as motion. Both types of batteries can be used for LED work.

Premade battery holders are an excellent (and easy) way for cosplayers to power up their work and I recommend starting with these. Battery holders can be purchased to work with coin cell batteries or with AAA, AA, and nine-volt batteries. They usually come with a switch attached to the holder or on separate wire lines.

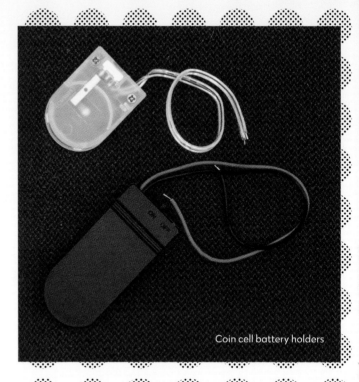

Coin cell battery holders

TIP Know that the more LEDs you put on a circuit, the more power they will draw. The number of LED lights that can be used at full brightness varies. Most LED packaging indicates the amount of power in volts drawn by each light or each string of lights. Check the amount of voltage they draw, multiply by the number of lights, and purchase the right battery to handle it.

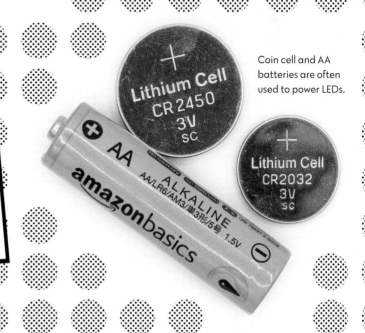

Coin cell and AA batteries are often used to power LEDs.

Soldering

Soldering is a technique where you join two or more electronic parts together by melting solder over the joined area. Once the solder cools, your pieces are joined together. This was the technique that I was most nervous about when I started adding lighting to my builds. In reality, it's not that bad. If you have adequate tools and space to do the work, you'll find it an easy and exciting addition to your cosplay skills. The solder wire has a low melting point, making it easy to activate the solder with a soldering tool. The solder tool does not melt wires or other items that you plan to solder; just be careful where you point the tip.

Soldering in action!

Testing my connection

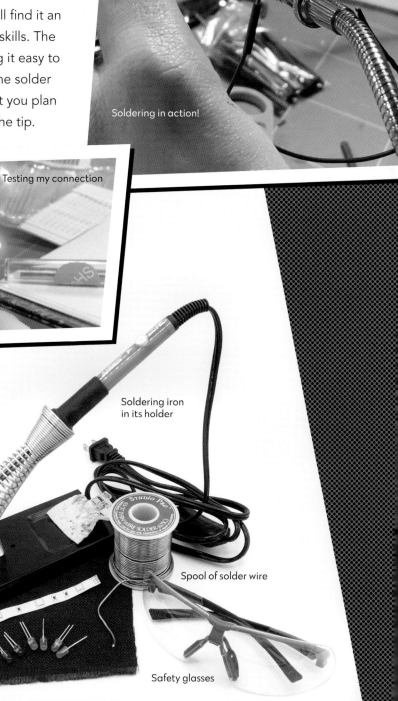

Soldering iron in its holder

Spool of solder wire

MY ENTIRE LED AND SOLDERING KIT

LED lights

Safety glasses

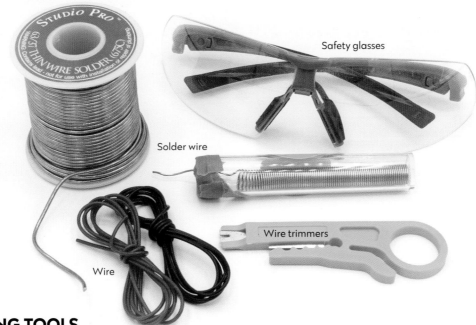

Safety glasses

Solder wire

Wire trimmers

Wire

SOLDERING TOOLS

SOLDER is a metal alloy used to create a permanent bond between electrical parts. Solder is available in several varieties, but for our purposes you should choose lead-free rosin core solder. Solder is sold in a few different diameters, but smaller diameter wire is better for working with small circuitry, such as LED lights. Usually sold in a spool, you use a soldering iron to melt the solder and join your connection. Allow the solder to cool and the electrical components are permanently adhered.

A **SOLDERING IRON** is a hand tool with a heated tip used to melt solder. For the work you will be doing with LEDs you will want a pen style soldering iron in the 15W to 30W range. Most irons come with interchangeable tips and for small circuit work you will want a conical tip. Be sure the soldering iron you purchase comes with this tip. When using a soldering iron remember, safety first! The tip gets extremely hot and can cause burns or fires. Be sure to place the soldering iron back in the stand when not in use and never touch the tip.

A **WIRE CUTTER AND STRIPPER TOOL** is used to cut wire and strip the ends of wire to allow for an electrical connection.

TWEEZERS help you grab hold of small wires or items needing soldering.

HELPING HANDS are very helpful when soldering. They feature a base with two or more flexible arms topped with small clamps to hold each component that needs soldering, allowing you to keep your hands free to hold the soldering iron and solder.

Keep a **WET SPONGE** or **BRASS SPONGE** on hand to clean your soldering tip after each use.

SAFETY GLASSES are essential to protect your eyes from accidental splatters.

ADEQUATE VENTILATION is likewise essential because soldering can produce harmful vapors.

Wear a **RESPIRATOR MASK** to protect yourself from any harmful vapors.

HOW TO SOLDER WIRES TOGETHER

Before you begin, heat up your soldering iron and melt a bit of solder over the tip. This is called tinning the tip and will extend the life of your tip.

1. Clip the electrical components that you plan to solder to the helping hands tool.

2. Using the flexible arms, arrange the pieces to be joined close together and heat up the soldering iron.

3. Position the soldering iron tip close to the wires that you want to melt together and gently touch the wires to heat them.

4. Touch the solder to the heated wires and allow the solder to melt and flow over the connection. You do not need a lot of solder.

5. Once the solder cools, your wires will be conjoined.

6. Clean the tip of the soldering iron. I use a wet sponge placed on a plate to clean it off.

COSPLAYER: Jedimanda
COSTUME: Ahsoka Tano from the Star Wars franchise LEDs are used to illuminate the light saber.

Planning my circuitry to achieve the look I want and determine how much wire I'll need

Simple Circuitry

Now that you know a bit about LEDs, batteries, and soldering, let's connect them. To do basic circuitry work, you need to plan exactly what you are going to connect. I like to draw a layout consisting of my battery, the wires, and a single LED (see illustration). A single LED has two wires descending from the bulb: a long and a short leg. The long leg is called an anode and it is marked with a plus sign (+). The short leg is a cathode and it is marked with a negative sign (-). When attaching the wires, attach the positive side of the battery to the positive leg of the LED. Once all of this is soldered together, flip that switch on the battery pack, and let there be light!

After tackling a few single LED lights, you can go crazy. Explore using more LEDs and bigger circuitry, just keep in mind that more lights and power will require not just more battery power but the use of resistors to keep things running correctly. Jump online and learn more advanced circuitry so that your cosplay can glow bigger and brighter.

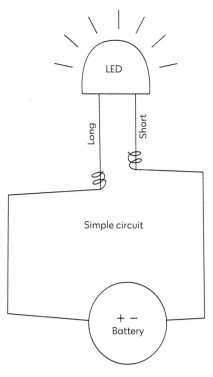

LED

Long   Short

Simple circuit

+ −
Battery

Incorporating Premade Lights into Your Costume

Most people think of Christmas lights as the only pre-made light strings available to work with, but this isn't true. Let me introduce you to my favorite lighting setup: *fairy lights*. Fairy lights are tiny LED lights that are amazingly bright when you turn them on. The LED bulbs are laced on a thin, flexible metal wire that you can wrap around anything and bend into any shape to create fairy lighting that is perfect for cosplay creation. Many fairy lights are battery powered either with a coin cell battery or packs requiring multiple batteries. Some also have a handheld remote to control the settings for color, light mode, and speed.

1. Combination
2. In wave
3. Sequential
4. Slo glo
5. Chasing/Flash
6. Slow fade
7. Twinkle/Flash
8. Steady on
9. Off

Fairy lights with a remote

You can purchase fairy lights at any craft store or online. Just make sure you know how many LEDs you need, the desired LED light strength, and the color of the LEDs before you order. Sometimes you can purchase smaller strands with fewer LED lights, which require less battery power.

Unlit fairy lights are concealed within my Captain Marvel mohawk

Lit fairy lights in my Captain Marvel mohawk

COSPLAYER: Jedimanda
COSTUME: Captain Marvel from Marvel Cinematic Universe

You can just switch these lights on and let them shine. They're easy to hide in your costume. Other larger circuits—like the one I made for my Anastasia crown and Captain Marvel helmet—require a more creative way to hide the battery pack.

You can use foam, thermoplastics, and lots of glue to conceal the battery packs practically anywhere. Keep in mind that rechargeable battery packs might emit heat. Test your battery pack to see if it does emit heat before wearing them or installing them in a part of your costume that will be in direct contact with your body. Bring lots of backup batteries with you when you head to a convention, so you are ready for the convention floor!

Placing the fairy lights under the foam.

Checking out the brightness of the lights in the foam.

COSPLAYER: Jedimanda
COSTUME: Ahsoka Tano from the
Star Wars franchise

ALTERING THRIFTED AND PREMADE ACCESSORIES

Saving money and time is a massive "want" in the game of cosplay. I can't tell you how many times I've made something from scratch to then turn around and tell myself that it would have been easier to just buy the thing. As a craftsmanship-type cosplayer, for some reason, I feel like I must make every single thing. You do not have to make everything in your cosplay unless you are competing in a craftsmanship competition, which is a different story. Make existing clothing pieces work for you! Let's chat about some of my favorite tips and tricks for altering accessories.

COSPLAYER: Jedimanda
COSTUME: Kitana from *Mortal Kombat 11* Thrifted boots were the perfect base to build from for this costume.
Photo by World of Gwendana

Where Can I Find These Items?

The short answer to where you can find premade or thrifted items to alter is: anywhere! Look in your closet, your local thrift store, Amazon, even the bargain bins at your local department store. Put on your adventuring outfit and go hunting. My favorite places to hit up are Goodwill, local charity thrift stores, Target, and even the clearance sections at Macy's. Depending on what you are looking for, thrift stores are often the biggest win. I also love to shop at online thrift stores; ThredUp is my favorite. ThredUp is just a big ole online thrift store with incredibly inexpensive prices on gently-used and some-times brand-new items. I always start at ThredUp when I am searching for shoes, belts, bags, and basic cloth-ing pieces like leggings and undershirts. I believe their prices are great for cosplay repurposing and reusing. Other online sites like eBay, Depop, and Poshmark are also great online sites for thrifting.

No matter where you shop, make sure you check out the item thoroughly before buying it. This is a little more difficult with online sites, but they usually allow returns. Look for holes, discoloration, and signs of dry rot. It de-pends on what you are hunting for—sometimes broken or problem areas can be fixed. Don't forget to clean and/or wash the item before beginning the altering process. Now let's get into some of my favorite tips and tricks for altering thrifted or premade accessories.

For my Mabel from *Animal Crossing* cosplay, I used clothes from my closet and a handmade apron, and handmade ears.

COSPLAYER: Jedimanda
COSTUME: Evie from *The Mummy*

I added belt loops to a thrifted skirt for my Evie cosplay.

Belts

Belts are one of the many items that I always thrift. There are so many options already out there, and they are easily altered. Recycled leather belts and even faux leather belts are easy to paint. I tend to reuse belts for multiple cosplays. I also like to thrift belts for their buckles. More and more cosplay designs are getting creative with belt buckles, and recycled buckles make a great base to build around.

Bags and Purses

Depending on what you are looking for, thrift stores can have lots of options. I like to hunt for small bags that I can work into my costumes to use as hidden pockets. Thrifted or premade bags are a great option since making custom bags can be very time-consuming. Cutting corners here can be a big help in the long run. Waist packs are some of my favorite pieces to find. You can easily work these into a costume for extra storage. My first book, *Creative Cosplay*, includes a full tutorial on how to make your own!

TIP You can use spot cleaner to clean up thrifted bags and breathe new life into them. Bags and purses are also easy to repaint with the proper paint and surface prep (see Fabric paint, page 56).

COSPLAYER: Jedimanda
COSTUME: Captain Marvel from Marvel Cinematic Universe
A thrifted lunchbox was the perfect base for creating Captain Marvel's Fonz lunch box
Photo by David Ngo

Printed image to adhere to the lunchbox for Captain Marvel.

Gloves

Gloves are hands down my least favorite thing to make. For some reason, I just really dislike making them. The frustrations of tight corners, stretchy fabric, and multiple mock-ups add up, so I usually consult premade glove options first. I comb Amazon hoping to find what I need and usually, I do! The best part is that gloves are easy to alter; you can cut them up, repaint them, and even add scraps of different fabrics and trims.

You can try acrylic wash techniques to achieve an easy weathered look. An acrylic wash is a mix of water and acrylic paint. Usually, I start with a two-to-one ratio, with two parts water to one part acrylic paint. Adding more water dilutes the paint, giving you a more washed-out look. I used this method for my Ahsoka Tano gloves, and it worked perfectly! Another easy option is to purchase short gloves and add cuffs or sleeves to extend the design of the glove. Gloves are easy to alter but tough to make, but I guarantee you will find an option that works for you.

Ahsoka Tano gloves, repainted with attached thermoplastic details.

Distressing Ahsoka's gloves with acrylic paint.

COSPLAYER: Jedimanda
COSTUME: Ahsoka Tano from the Star Wars franchise

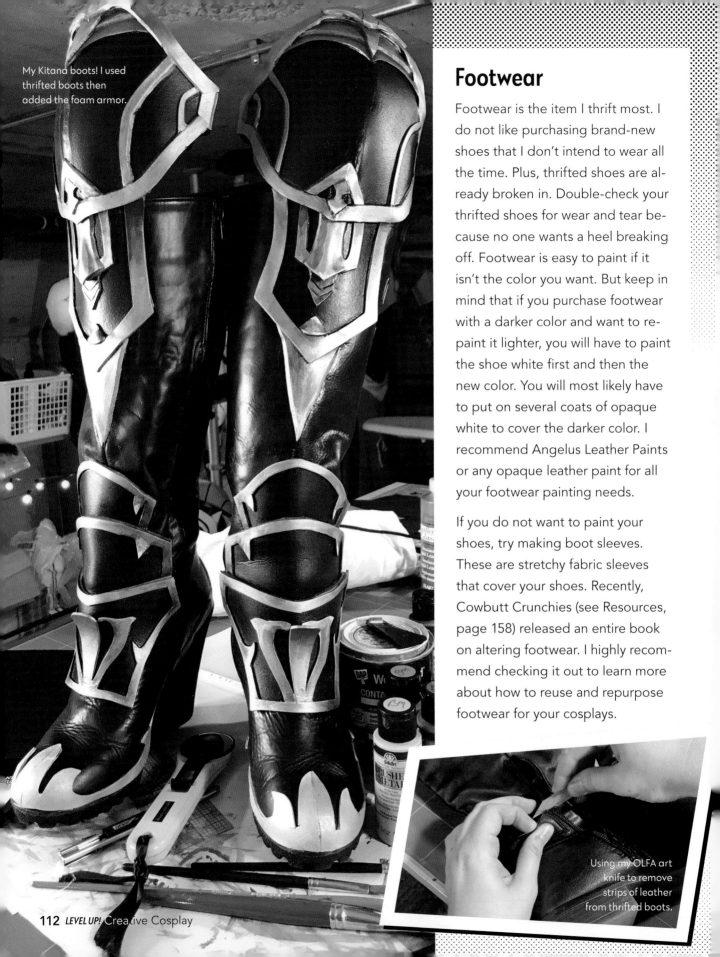

My Kitana boots! I used thrifted boots then added the foam armor.

Footwear

Footwear is the item I thrift most. I do not like purchasing brand-new shoes that I don't intend to wear all the time. Plus, thrifted shoes are already broken in. Double-check your thrifted shoes for wear and tear because no one wants a heel breaking off. Footwear is easy to paint if it isn't the color you want. But keep in mind that if you purchase footwear with a darker color and want to repaint it lighter, you will have to paint the shoe white first and then the new color. You will most likely have to put on several coats of opaque white to cover the darker color. I recommend Angelus Leather Paints or any opaque leather paint for all your footwear painting needs.

If you do not want to paint your shoes, try making boot sleeves. These are stretchy fabric sleeves that cover your shoes. Recently, Cowbutt Crunchies (see Resources, page 158) released an entire book on altering footwear. I highly recommend checking it out to learn more about how to reuse and repurpose footwear for your cosplays.

Using my OLFA art knife to remove strips of leather from thrifted boots.

Hats

Hats are another great accessory to buy premade. I don't recommend thrifting them unless you can confirm that they are clean or that you will be able to sanitize and clean them yourself. The more creative your hat style is going to be, the more expensive it will be to purchase; however, basic hats are cheap, and you can easily build on top of them. So start with a hat base and build from that. You can add trims and fabrics to cover the hat, then throw on all the embellishments you want. You can also paint or hand-dye hat bases. I recommend acrylic paint and acrylic paint washes. Do a spot test first on the underside of the hat, and then go for it!

Other Items to Alter or Thrift

As I said earlier, you do not have to make everything you wear for cosplay. Help yourself and save some time by purchasing small pieces that can help you make progress on your cosplay. I love purchasing new leggings to wear under my ball gowns or even thrifting an entire costume. Have fun, and don't be afraid to explore those thrift stores.

TIP

A closet cosplay is a costume you assemble entirely from items already in your closet (or maybe ones already at a thrift store near you)!

Also, try thrifting different parts of your props. Take a gander through the Amazon lightning deals or Goodwill's home decor; you never know what you might find. When I decided to make the Nadja doll for my Nadja cosplay from *What We Do in the Shadows*, I knew I didn't want to make the entire prop. I purchased a cheap ventriloquist dummy from Amazon and promptly took off its head. I created a new head for the doll and dressed it up. Making the doll only took half the time it would have because I cut out some basic work by buying that item. It might not have been thrifted, but it worked.

The doll base I altered to use for my Nadja doll prop

COSPLAYER: Jedimanda
COSTUME: Nadja and Nadja doll from
What We Do in the Shadows

MAKEUP!

This chapter is all about daily convention makeup and special effects make-up. I want to tell you that a lot of folks–no matter their chosen gender– wear makeup or skin care products of some sort at a convention. Cosplaying at conventions is practically theater. People dress up and show off in front of other people. You want to look your best, and you want your face to look just as fabulous as the amazing cosplay you made to wear; it adds to the confidence that your cosplay brings.

COSPLAYER: Jedimanda
COSTUME: Mileena from *Mortal Kombat 11*
Special effects using latex and prosthetics for Mileena's look

Basic Cosplay Convention Makeup and Skin Care

Makeup is genderless, and everyone can use it to protect their faces against harsh environments, including indoor convention center air and outdoor environments. You'll often find yourself outside in all kinds of weather doing your epic photoshoots.

Use makeup to help you feel confident and make those photographs turn out amazing. You will quickly find that many photographs tend to wash out the definition of your face. Sometimes it's the photographer's fault or the fault of the ugly convention carpet you are standing on. Unfortunately, a lot of convention centers have bad lighting and bad carpet colors that bounce odd colors onto your skin. (I'm talking to you, Indianapolis Convention Center.) Combined with the flashes that photographers use, your face can get washed out and result in an unflattering photo. Let's combat that with great makeup and skin care choices. Even if it's just a lovely lotion to prevent dryness, I recommend everyone pay attention to this chapter on makeup. Let's dive in!

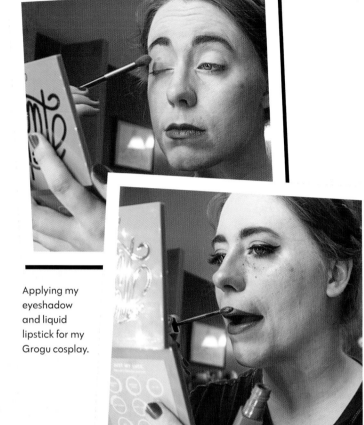

Applying my eyeshadow and liquid lipstick for my Grogu cosplay.

MY COSPLAY MAKEUP KIT!
My kit almost always contains a foundation brush, liquid lipstick, mascara, eyelashes, eyeshadow palette, face lotion, face primer, sunscreen, foundation, concealer, eyebrow gel, blush, and face powder.

Not everything mentioned in the Daily and Convention Makeup section (see page 118) is necessary, but for conventions, I use a lot of those items listed. Conventions can be very hot or really cold and dry. I need my makeup to last all day and help prevent too much sweating. Skin care products that you use to layer up are important. Using primers with a foundation and eyeshadow helps prevent creasing and running.

TIP

Carry blotting paper with you at an especially hot convention (Hello, Dragon Con) to help keep your makeup in place. Setting sprays and powders are also very helpful to set and keep makeup from melting off your face. Carry these products around with you throughout the day.

Building a collection of makeup bases takes time, and you will find that you like certain products better than others. Practice putting on your makeup before the convention. Even if it's just daily makeup with simple products, practice helps reduce your stress on convention day. Don't forget to wash and clean your brushes, sponges, and various applicators to keep everything fresh and clean. Remember that nothing is wrong with wearing makeup no matter who you are; we all just want to look and feel our best while in cosplay.

COSPLAYER: Jedimanda
COSTUME: Sabrina Spellman from *Chilling Adventures of Sabrina*
Sabrina's character needs everyday beauty makeup that tips the scale in a darker direction. I used a deeper hued lipstick and eye makeup to give her a slightly spooky glam look.

Sunscreen

Face lotion

CeraVe

Facial primer

SKIN CARE FAVES!

Facial serum

Night cream

Eye primer

DAILY AND CONVENTION MAKEUP

I believe daily makeup can be broken down into three categories: under skin care, color, and add-ons. This list includes types (not brands) of makeup.

Skin Care

FACE WASH to always start with a clean face

TONERS to help clean the skin and reduce the appearance of pores

LOTIONS AND MOISTURIZERS to protect and moisturize the skin

SERUMS to help retain moisture while delivering active ingredients targeting specific needs

PRIMERS to apply before makeup to help smooth textured skin

SUNSCREEN to protect the skin from the sun's ultraviolet rays that could damage skin

CONCEALER to conceal marks or blemishes

FOUNDATION in liquid, cream, or powder form, to serve as the final product before adding colors

Colors

The following products come in a variety of shades and colors.

BLUSH to help enhance the natural color of the skin

CONTOUR, both a technique and a range of products, to define and sculpt facial structure

BROW COLORS to enhance and shape eyebrows

EYESHADOW to draw attention to the eyes using a wide variety of colors

EYELINER to enhance and elongate the depth of the eye

MASCARA to lengthen, darken, and thicken eyelashes

LIP PRODUCTS to enhance the lips with different colors of lip gloss, lip liner, lipstick, and liquid lipstick

HIGHLIGHTER to highlight certain areas of the face

My favorites for adding color: blush, eyeliner, eyeshadow palettes, a variety of liquid lipsticks, mascara, eyebrow gel, and liquid eyeliner

Applying blush to my cheekbones

Drawing face paint onto my neck to complete my "Glam Porg" look, inspired by the Porg in *Star Wars Episode VIII: The Last Jedi.*

COSPLAYER: Jedimanda
COSTUME: Porg, inspired by the Star Wars franchise
Wearing Beauty Porg makeup

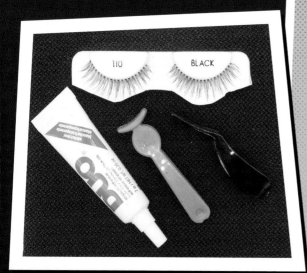

Add-ons

EYELASHES used to thicken, exaggerate, or add extension to eyelashes

FAUX NAILS used to enhance nails

Miscellaneous

BLOTTING PAPER to remove oil from your skin throughout the day

SETTING SPRAYS to set your makeup so it will hold for the whole day

SETTING POWDERS help to set liquid and cream-based makeups to prevent running

BRUSHES, SPONGES, AND VARIOUS APPLICATORS to apply makeup

FAVORITE PRODUCTS RECOMMENDED BY MY COSPLAY FRIENDS

My go-to foundation for cosplay is Amazonian clay from Tarte. It's full coverage, lightweight, and is SPF 15!
—Casey Renee Cosplay

I love bringing facial mask jars to conventions, especially Lush's Mask of Magnaminty! Wearing heavy cosplay makeup for days in a row is rough on your skin, so taking the time to indulge in a soothing or hydrating mask is the perfect way to help get it back on track!
—Cowbutt Crunchies Cosplay

Urban Decay's All Nighter Setting Spray is a MUST when wanting makeup to stay on all day at a con. —Captain Kaycee Cosplay

I really love using a combo of Fenty Beauty Pro Filt'r loose powder and Kryolan Fixing Spray. They help to both set my makeup and lock it in place for hours of con floor time. I have oily skin, so I need all the help I can get! —April Gloria

My favorite makeup product would have to be lipsticks from Fenty Beauty. These lipsticks have been the best match for my skin tone, and I love that the brand promotes diversity. Not only does applying the lipstick indicate that the whole makeup portion is done and I've successfully transformed into the character (hopefully!), but it also gives me a confidence boost in my facial expressions practice. Plus, the variety of colors easily adds to the aesthetic without needing to put much else on. —Nyvedna Productions

COSPLAYER: Jedimanda
COSTUME: Yennefer of Vengerberg from *The Witcher*
This character requires a combination of special
effects makeup and beauty makeup.

Basic Body Painting

There are a lot of fictional characters with unusual skin colors. From a blue alien to a red demon, let's go over how to body paint! Conquering body paint takes practice and patience.

COSPLAYER: Jedimanda
COSTUME: Sally from *The Nightmare Before Christmas*
Sally uses basic body painting techniques that anyone can learn

GREAT MAKEUP TAKES PRACTICE

I will never forget my first foray into body paint—it's story time, y'all. My first time being Ahsoka Tano for a convention was in 2015, and I was guesting for Wizard World Louisville. I had a new costume for Ahsoka that I had just finished the night before, and I didn't get a chance to play with my body paint application. This was the first time I had used water-activated body paint, and I thought I could add it on my body with a beauty blender, a.k.a. a makeup sponge that you wet. The morning of the day I wore Ahsoka, I woke up with a great attitude that was quickly crushed when my paint would not stay on my face. I didn't realize that applying water-activated makeup with a wet sponge just kept removing the paint. So in my stressed moment, I started to cry, and since the crying added more moisture to my face, my paint continued to run. My boyfriend and friend brought me a cookie which helped me to calm down. Once the sponge had dried a bit, I was able to apply my makeup, allowing the paint to go on and stick. The moral of the story is: cookies fix everything, always practice and test your body paint before show time, and don't use a wet sponge to apply water-activated body paint.

Using my favorite Mehron water-activated paints for my Ahsoka Tano cosplay, I can't recommend them enough.

COSPLAYER: Jedimanda
COSTUME: Ahsoka Tano from the Star-Wars franchise

SKIN CARE BEFORE BODY PAINTING

Before you start body painting, you need to consider skin prep. I don't load up my face with a lot of lotions, serums, and primers because you need the paint to stick. I recommend a good daily lotion and a primer (see Skin Care, page 118). The primer helps smooth out your face texture to get it ready for the paint. If you are painting more than your face—like your shoulders, arms, and chest—I do recommend applying lotion to your skin.

My Mehron water activated paint palettes with the brushes I use.

TYPES OF BODY PAINT

Okay, hold on to your pants! There are a lot of body paint options. Body paint comes in either a single color or a larger palette of several liquid or cream paints. I've broken types of body paint into four types: water activated, alcohol activated, cream based, and greasepaint. Choose the paint based on the look you want and how much you are willing to spend. I've used them all, and I hope I can help steer you in the best direction for whatever you are planning. Let's get into it.

TIP

A variety of brushes, sponges, and a water basin is about all you need to apply the paints.

TIP

You will probably want to use a combination of setting items for your body paint. Once your body paint is dry, apply colorless setting powder with a giant brush first and then setting spray. Your paint will last throughout the day.

Mehron setting spray

Ben Nye setting powder

NYX powder

Mehron setting powder

My chosen setting powders and sprays to use for face paints

Face paint brushes with
Mehron water activated paints

Water Activated

My favorite brands include Mehron, Ben Nye, Diamond FX, Graftobian, Kryolan, TAG, and Wolfe FX.

Water-activated body paint is a soft glycerin-based paint. I use this paint the most because it's easy to apply and it looks vibrant on my skin. These paints are usually the least expensive and are easy to find.

I apply this paint with a brush. You can control the amount of water much better with a brush than with a sponge. I recommend keeping a variety of brushes on hand, along with a container for water (but you don't need a lot of water). A wide flat brush and a large fluffy brush are ideal for painting the main color application and laying down the color all over the body. You can use sponges if you prefer; I just find it difficult to control the amount of water with a sponge.

COSPLAYER: Jedimanda
COSTUME: Sally from *The Nightmare Before Christmas* Water based paint was perfect for Sally because it layers really well, which was key to capturing Sally's look.

Adding the white water activated face paint for my Ahsoka Tano makeup

Adding the iconic orange paint for my Ahsoka Tano.

Putting contour on my Ahsoka Tano makeup to sculpt out my face

When you are ready, dip your brush first into the water then into the paint, swirl the paint around the palette with the brush, and then paint your face. You will get the hang of how much water and how much paint to use once you get to painting.

This paint dries quickly, but depending on the color you are looking for, you might need to paint multiple layers. Water-activated paint is easy to layer, but you do need to let the layers dry between applications. Once your day is done, the paint is extremely easy to remove; just wipe it off with water.

Keep in mind that if you tend to sweat, especially at a convention, you might want to carry touch-up paint with you. I get sweaty in costume, and I swear it's my superpower: instantly when I'm in costume, I start to sweat. Water-activated paint is great for all-day wear at a convention, but it doesn't last as long outside. To help the paint stay, apply colorless setting powder with a big powder brush all over your body, and you will be golden.

TIP Wax-based paints are water activated too, but I only use them for line work. If you need crisp clean lines, grab a long, thin brush and use wax-based paint on top of your base paint job. This paint is ideal for small details and clean lines. Great brands for wax-based paints are Wolfe FX and TAG.

Alcohol Activated

The most popular alcohol-activated paint is Skin Illustrator. Other brands include Endura from European Body Art, Temptu Pro's Dura and Special Effects colors, Graftobian, and Pro Aiir. A little of this paint goes a long way, so don't let the price scare you.

Various alcohol- and water-activated paints that I apply with my airbrush

Alcohol-activated paints are, in my opinion, the next step up from water-activated paints. For some reason, I used to think that alcohol-activated paints were more difficult to work with. Turns out, they are not. They are very easy to use because instead of dipping your brush in water to paint, you dip it in alcohol—easy! Alcohol-activated paints come in palette and liquid forms. You can apply this makeup with a brush, sponge, and most commonly with an airbrush. Most people flock to alcohol-activated paints for their longevity (they will stay on longer) and because they are more sweatproof than water-activated paints. However, in high movement areas like creases in the skin, the paint does clump up and fall off. Just be aware of that, and be careful in those areas.

Alcohol-activated paint palettes are usually used for very translucent looks. They are good for "under the skin" effects like bruises, simple cuts, and opaque details. This palette must be activated with 99 percent isopropyl alcohol. For some reason, this alcohol is expensive, but it comes in a large container that will last a long time. You don't need a lot of alcohol to get the paints going. These paints dry fast and are great for detail work; they can be used on top of water-activated paints.

Alcohol-activated paint tends to create a seamless, brushless look. I love using it to apply face paint for my new Ahsoka Tano from *The Mandalorian* cosplay. Since Ahsoka Tano's look has a very opaque skin color, it is important to minimize visible brush strokes. I use liquid paint applied with an airbrush to achieve this look. If you want a brushless and seamless finish to your body paint, I recommend this method.

COSPLAYER: Jedimanda
COSTUME: Ahsoka Tano from the Star Wars franchise
Alcohol-activated paint tends to create a seamless, brushless look. I love using it to apply face paint for my new Ahsoka Tano from *The Mandalorian.*

Apply the paint with an airbrush in a well-ventilated area. Practice first on the back of your hand to get the hang of the pressure and trigger of the brush, then try airbrushing your chest and neck. Take your time and practice; you'll soon get the hang of airbrushing body paint. If you can, have a buddy on hand to help.

To remove alcohol-activated paint, rub your skin (both body and face) with baby oil. Let the oil sit on your skin for a couple of minutes, then just wipe it off with a towel or hop in the shower and rinse it off—but you still need to scrub your skin a bit. Several brands offer removal liquids that also work well.

Cream Based

My favorite brands include Ben Nye, Mehron, and Graftobian.

I use cream-based paint for some details but not necessarily directly on my skin for cosplay. People typically consider cream-based paint for the *bruise wheel*. The bruise wheel is a common, small palette used for fake special effects like bruising, cuts, and skin abrasions. There are cream-based paints almost everywhere and in every color. They blend well, and you can use a brush or sponge to apply them. One of their biggest downsides is that they take forever to dry. Accidentally touching cream-based paint could smear it, but if you apply it well, the makeup will stay. Using a final setting powder also helps keep the makeup on. I don't recommend using this for your entire body or entire face; instead, use it for details and small makeup designs. Remove it with a makeup wipe or facial wash, then rinse and pat dry with a towel.

The only greasepaint I own, Mehron's Clown White greasepaint and the sponges I use to apply greasepaint

Greasepaint

My favorite brands include Mehron, Ben Nye, Kryolan, and ProFace.

Greasepaint is the third wheel of the body paint world. No one likes to use it for cosplay except for very specific applications. Greasepaint was one of the first makeup types designed for the theater, and it was created to withstand the heat of the lights on stage. This paint is quite thick and does not dry. If you touch your face after putting on this makeup, it will smear—I promise. You can set it with powder to help your skin look more matte, but it still will not dry. Apply it thinly with a sponge or brush; a little bit goes a long way. I use a standard foundation makeup sponge. Since greasepaint is easy to smear, it's easy to remove: just wipe it off with a makeup wipe.

There are good uses for greasepaint. I use it for my Queen Amidala looks. I love it because it does not run, and you only need a small amount. I used to use water-activated paint, but that was a problem because I sweat like crazy under all the layers of my Queen Amidala cosplay. This makeup works great for me, as long as I don't touch my face.

My cream-based makeup kit includes a sponge, cotton swabs, brushes, Mehron ProColorRing Bruise, and Mehron cream stick in black.

COSPLAYER: Jedimanda
COSTUME: Queen Amidala from the Star Wars franchise. I used cream based makeup for Amidala because it is difficult to achieve a flawless look using white water- and alcohol-activated paints.

COSPLAYER: Jedimanda
COSTUME: Darth Maul from
the Star Wars Franchise
Darth Maul is a deceptively
easy design. Black and red are
standard palette colors, no
blending is required!

BEGINNER KIT

Building a kit is the first step into special effects makeup. It's hard to know where to start, but a body paint kit doesn't have to have every color in the universe. I suggest getting the primary colors, black, white, and whichever main color you need. Water-activated paints are your cheapest option, but I suggest buying a good brand. No one wants thin, cheap paints. Grab a variety of brushes, sponges, and a water basin too. Now that you have a small kit, try out some easy designs first. Start small with designs that use colors that don't require mixing. Once you have a look you want to try, start dipping your brush into the paint. Apply the colors to your skin using a smaller brush, then try applying with a larger brush. There is no right or wrong way to apply paint to your skin just watch the ratio of water to paint if you are using water-activated paint. The more water on the brush with less paint, the less opaque your application will be. If you are using alcohol-activated paints, watch the amount you place on the brush as well. A little goes a long way with the alcohol on your brush, play around and you will find the magic ratio. For greasepaint and cream, same rules apply, just watch the amount you are picking up with your brush or sponge. Body painting is all about practice and getting comfortable with the paint.

Special Effects Makeup

We have covered body painting; now let's go over the basics of special effects make-up! I define special effects (SFX) makeup as makeup that uses prosthetics or other materials to create a three-dimensional effect. Doing SFX makeup can be a quick and easy application with a premade, purchased piece, or it could be a multiday adventure by making everything you need to apply to your face. It's all up to you.

COSPLAYER: Jedimanda
COSTUME: Mileena from *Mortal Kombat 11*
Mileena has an iconic smile that doesn't exist in nature. It was up to me to take on the challenge of making the prosthetic for my look. I used moldable plastic for the teeth, tissues and cottonballs to build up the piece, all combined with a lot of liquid latex layers. I then finishing the application by painting and adding fake blood.

BASIC PROSTHETICS MATERIALS, TECHNIQUES, AND TOOLS

First, what is an SFX prosthetic? It's an artificial body part made with sculpting, molding, and casting techniques to create advanced cosmetic effects. SFX prosthetics have been used in moviemaking since the early-twentieth century to create special and sometimes scary looks for the actors. *The Wolf Man (1941)*, *Frankenstein (1931)*, and *The Phantom of the Opera (1925)* are some of the first films that used prosthetics. Applied with a variety of glues, layered up with latex, and painted to create an illusion, basic SFX prosthetic and makeup work is so much fun, and it helps create an amazing finishing touch for any cosplay.

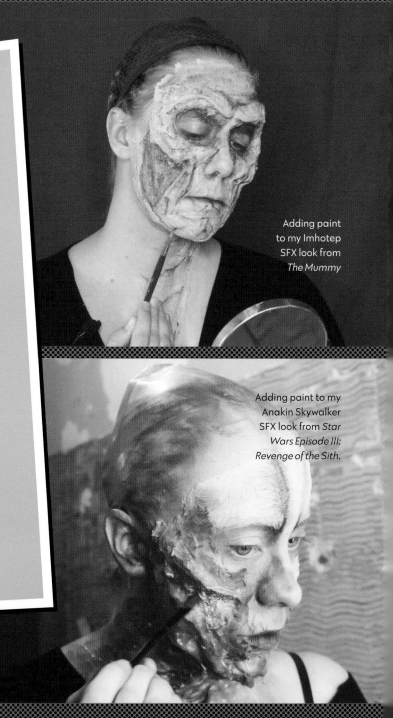

Adding paint to my Imhotep SFX look from *The Mummy*

Adding paint to my Anakin Skywalker SFX look from *Star Wars Episode III: Revenge of the Sith.*

My simple SFX makeup kit: craft sticks, sponges, oats, cream-based paint palette, a bottle of liquid latex, cotton swabs, cotton balls, fake blood, and a flat brush

TIP

SFX makeup can be intimidating, but when you break it down to simple steps it becomes completely doable. As a fellow cosplayer once said, all you have to do is "Build the thing. … Apply the thing. … Paint the thing."

Special Effects Makeup Kit

As with body paint, building a kit for special effects makeup work takes time and experimentation. Here are the items that I have in my kit.

To create prosthetics you'll need:

LIQUID LATEX, one of the main ingredients for basic SFX work in makeup, apply in thin layers, let it dry, and go again building upon the layers to create a surface

COTTON BALLS, a bulk medium to help build up the sculpted piece

TISSUES, my favorite texture building medium with latex

PALETTES a surface to make a prosthetic, if needed

To create and apply the SFX you'll need:

BRUSHES, a common applicator

SPONGES for applying the makeup

Q-TIPS to use as a good disposable applicator

CRAFT STICKS for mixing and applying

SCALPELS or **PALETTE KNIVES** for applying latex and layering

ADHESIVES such as spirit gum, Pros-Aide adhesive, or tapes to apply the prosthetic piece to your skin

To finish the look you'll want:

A **HAIR DRYER** to speed up drying time for latex pieces

PLASTIC CONTAINERS to be used as basins, mixing bowl, or extra space

FAUX BLOOD of multiple textures will help give you many different "gore" looks

PAINTS, cream based, alcohol activated, and/or water-activated paints

PHOTO JOURNAL OF BUILDING MY MILEENA MASK!

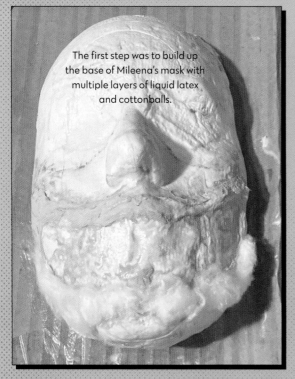

The first step was to build up the base of Mileena's mask with multiple layers of liquid latex and cottonballs.

Once I finished making the teeth, I added them to the piece then layered more liquid latex and cotton balls for bulk.

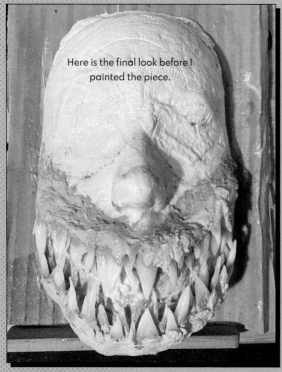

Here is the final look before I painted the piece.

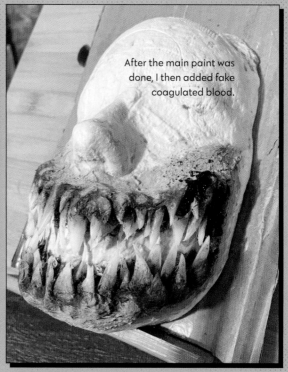

After the main paint was done, I then added fake coagulated blood.

Liquid Latex

Liquid latex should be a staple in everyone's SFX makeup kit. Liquid latex is 33 percent latex, 66 percent water, and 1 percent ammonia, and it comes premade and ready to use. If you choose to use this, please check for a latex allergy by dabbing some on the back of your hand. This product will harm the skin of anyone with a latex allergy.

Latex dries clear but builds up a lot over multiple layers, and it is the base for almost all prosthetic work. Layering liquid latex with different mediums can build up a structure to sculpt and then paint. You can apply liquid latex directly on your skin or on a separate surface. You can even add mediums like tissues, cotton balls, oats, and dry cereal to build up texture. It may seem weird, but these textures are very effective. Applying liquid latex is easy too; you can use Q-tips, craft sticks, makeup spatulas, brushes, and makeup sponges.

The latex needs to dry completely between layers and before painting. I suggest using cream-based or alcohol-activated paints applied with sponges and brushes to paint latex. One of my favorite aspects of liquid latex is that it also acts as glue. You can use liquid latex to create any look you want! There are other mediums like foam latex, gelatin, and silicone, but for a beginner, liquid latex is all you need.

FINISHING TOUCHES
Once you add the latex piece to your body, you need to feather the edges to blend it into your skin. I recommend using layers of tissues and latex brushed onto the edges of the piece. Let it dry then use some foundation or body paint to blend the prosthetic into your skin.

COSPLAYER: Jedimanda
COSTUME: Imhotep from *The Mummy*
I recreated one of the many makeup looks from *The Mummy*. This one was especially challenging because in the actual film, this look is mainly a computer generated special effect. I challenged myself to recreate the look without the aid of a computer and gave it a shot. It looks great!

Using a sponge, I am applying liquid latex on top of built up texture I created using toilet paper and cotton balls.

Mediums

If you are making a latex prosthetic piece, you need a medium to help layer up the piece. You can use tissues, cotton balls, toilet paper, and more to achieve the shape, depth, and appearance you need.

To add a medium, tear it into small pieces, lay down a layer of liquid latex on whichever surface you're using to build your piece (your face, a face mold, or a flat surface), then lay the tissues or other medium on top. Let it dry, and you've built up layers! Experiment and crumple up the tissues or throw in some cotton balls for more structure. Just keep layering to build up the piece. If you are making a fake injury, cuts, or burns, you need to choose your mediums wisely. I've used oats and even dry cereal to mimic the texture of gore within injuries!

Applying SFX gel for my Anakin Skywalker makeup. SFX gel is a gelatin-based product usually used to portray scarring and skin distortions.

Applying liquid latex on top of tissue paper to create the look for Imhotep.

Applicators

I use a variety of applicators to apply my SFX work including palette knives, sponges, brushes, and even Q-tips. To sculpt liquid latex, I use palette knives. Palette knives are great for applying liquid latex to your skin or for applying thickly. The latex peels off the tool easily when dry, allowing you to use the knives over and over. Foundation sponges (both rectangular and circular) are good to use for applying liquid latex, but the latex will build up in the sponge and you will need to throw it away after use. Brushes can be the best option for applying liquid latex because you can more precisely control the application. However, the latex can build up quickly on a brush and they can't be reused.

Dryer, Paint, and Glues

Most of the time, liquid latex dries quickly so you don't have to wait long to add additional layers. When you just can't wait, use a hairdryer to help it dry quicker!

You can use all kinds of paint on top of latex, but I tend to keep cream-based and alcohol-activated paints in my SFX tool kit to use on top of latex. Those types of paint are less likely to soak into the latex because there is no water added to activate the paint. I have also seen people use multiple eyeshadow palettes and water-activated palettes to good effect, so experiment with different paints; it's part of the journey. As long as it sticks and it works, it's painted.

Glues are extremely important because you often need to adhere a prosthetic directly onto your body and safety is always a consideration. I use liquid latex and Pros-Aide adhesive as glues. Liquid latex is the better choice for basic applications and does keep my piece on my skin throughout the day. For longer convention days when my piece needs to stay in place and not move, or for areas of the body that will move a lot, such as the mouth, neck, and arm area, I prefer medical-grade Pros-Aide adhesive.

Gluing on my Mileena teeth with spirit gum and pressing to hold

Adding fake blood to my Mileen teeth using a paintbrush

REMOVING SFX

RIP IT! Just kidding. But really, though—if you applied the prosthetic with latex you can just peel it off. If it is difficult to remove, rubbing alcohol will help remove latex stuck to your facial or body hair. Use a cotton pad or cotton ball dipped in alcohol and run it over the edges, and the prosthetic edges will loosen. When you are removing the piece, go slow, since your hair might come up with it. If you used Pros-Aide adhesive, I suggest using their solvent to help loosen the glue.

Once you remove the piece, you can save it if you want! I tend to keep all of my custom prosthetics. Just trim up the edges so it looks fresh the next time you reapply the piece and clean it carefully with a damp cloth. Store it in a clean, cool, dry space like a plastic box, away from direct sunlight.

COSPLAYER: Jedimanda
COSTUME: Mileena from *Mortal Kombat 11*
At the end of my convention day I'll have to tackle the challenge of removing my prosthetic smile and storing it carefully for reuse.

Applying April Gloria's Zombie Taylor Swift makeup using a premade prosthetic

Making vs. Buying Prosthetics

If you've read all of this and decided that there is absolutely no way you're making a prosthetic piece, there are lots of pre-made options available. If you think it's too much time, too much money, too much goo: don't worry! Just walk through any Halloween costume store and you will see a plethora of premade prosthetics. If you find that they are a bit stiff, not at all close to your skin color, or just a bit off, you can easily customize them! The price points are usually low, so you can purchase several and experiment. Cut them up, build on top of them using the methods described, or change the color with cream-based and alcohol-activated paints. Using premade pieces can save you time and effort, plus there is a lot to choose from. If you do not find what you need at your standard costume shop or if you simply want a higher quality premade piece, those exist too, just prepare to pay more. Check out online vendors or specialty Etsy shops for handmade foam and latex prosthetics. A simple search using the term cosplay prosthetics will provide a world of options.

COSPLAYER: Cowbutt Crunchies Cosplay
COSTUME: Crowley from *Good Omens*
Colored contacts gave the final touch
needed to complete Crowley's look.
Photo by Amie Photos

Cosplay Contacts

Cosplay contacts are a bit of a headache. I don't use them. I wear contacts daily, and I don't have the funds for prescription cosplay contacts. However, you absolutely can get contacts for cosplay. If you choose to do so, I have a couple of very important tips for you. Contact lenses are not one-size-fits-all. The first tip is to purchase your contacts through an FDA-approved website (or one approved by an equivalent government health agency). Poorly-made contacts can damage your eyes, possibly permanently. The next tip is to get an eye exam and a prescription from a licensed eye doctor (ophthalmologist or optometrist), even if you feel your vision is perfect. When you are ordering the contacts, you will be asked the diameter, base curve, and prescription for each eye. Having a reliable prescription on file will enable you to order safe contacts.

TYPES OF COSPLAY CONTACTS

- **CIRCLE LENSES** are the common, colored contacts that change the color of the iris.

- **SCLERA CONTACTS** cover the entire eyeball; they are completely black or white.

- **MESH CONTACTS** have a mesh circle that helps blur out the iris and the pupil.

- **NATURAL CONTACTS** have a hint of color.

There are so many contacts to choose from; just be sure to order from a legitimate website with well-reviewed brands. Some good sites to choose from are Gothika, PinkyParadise, Honeycolor, and Uniqso.

Maintaining your contacts is easy. You need a good clean case and plenty of contact solution in each contact holding area. Keep your contacts moist and check them often to see if they need more contact solution. Don't let your contacts dry out.

CONVENTION COSPLAY REPAIR AND UPKEEP KITS

There is something everyone needs to have in their convention bags: a good repair/upkeep kit. I have used my kit so many times at conventions, and I keep adding more items to my bag. We put so much time into our cosplays; if something breaks on the convention floor, we need to be able to fix it.

COSPLAYERS: Left to right, Terieri Cosplay, Ilabelle Cosplay, and Cowbutt Crunchies Cosplay
COSTUMES: Murdoc, Noodle, and 2D from the Gorillaz
Photo by Sam Saturn

COSPLAYER: *Jedimanda*
COSTUME: Kitana from *Mortal Kombat 11*
Photo by World of Gwendana

COSPLAYER: *Jedimanda*
COSTUME: Queen Amidala from the Star Wars franchise
Behind the scenes fun at Star Wars Celebration 2019

I'll never forget the time I broke one of my props backstage at a competition. It was for the Crown Championships of Cosplay in March of 2020. I was dressed as Kitana and doing some backstage practicing. I had two handmade fan props that I created out of wood, Worbla, and fabric. I wanted to practice fanning them open, hoping to gain audience applause. During one of my practice flips, I dropped the fan and broke one of the blades. I had about five minutes before I went on stage, so I needed immediate help. Unfortunately, I did not have my repair kit with me—something I regret to this day. However, a stagehand came to the rescue. My handler asked him for some black gaffer tape to help hold it together enough that I could work it on stage. It worked, and I was so thankful for that tiny piece of gaffer tape. This goes to show how important it is to always have a kit on hand; you never know when accidents might happen.

I created two epic kits that I take to every convention. I am sharing my list so you can be completely prepared. This is a full list, so feel free to pick and choose what you want.

MY COSPLAY REPAIR KIT

Moleskin pads

Batteries

Hot glue gun

Safety pins

Thread

Scissors

Glue sticks

Needles

Duct tape

Costume Repair and Upkeep Kit

I keep my repair/upkeep kit as simple as possible so it is easily carried throughout the day. It usually includes:

SAFETY PINS (*various sizes*) for emergency reattachments

A **MINI SEWING KIT** with thread, needles, snips, and thimble for simple sewing repairs

SMALL HOT GLUE GUN WITH GLUE STICKS to reattach bits and pieces that are not fabric

DUCT TAPE or **GAFFER TAPE** for times when hot glue is not strong enough or will not bond

SMALL SCISSORS just in case

MOLESKIN for help with rough shoes (to prevent blisters)

ADHESIVE BANDAGES for blisters or small cuts

LINT ROLLER to keep everything looking neat

COSPLAYER: Jedimanda
COSTUME: Qi'ra from *Solo: A Star Wars Story*
Me as Qi'ra at Star Wars Celebration 2019.

Hair brush and mirror

Wig cap

Eyelash glue

Prosthetic adhesive
Pros-Aide

MY COSPLAY MAKEUP KIT

Hair pins

NYX MINERAL MINÉRALE
"Set It & Don't Fret It"
MATTE FINISHING POWDER
POUDRE DE FINITION MATIFIANTE

Setting powders

Wig tape

MAYBELLINE
Liquid lipstick

MATTE INK

Powder brush

Makeup Repair and Upkeep Kit

- Blotting paper

- Colorless setting powder

- Lipstick—your chosen color

- Small comb

- Hair pins, various sizes

- Hairspray (small can)

- Extra eyelash glue

- Contact solution (if applicable)

- Hair ties

COSPLAYER: Jedimanda
COSTUME: Qi'ra from *Solo: A Star Wars Story*
Interacting with a remote droid at Star Wars Celebration 2019.

WORKING IN THE COSPLAY WORLD

To wrap up this book, I want to tell you about an aspect of cosplay that many of us cosplayers do: marketing. We market ourselves online to promote our newest builds, show off our latest designs, or even to promote ourselves as guests at conventions. Having a social media presence or just an online presence isn't mandatory, but you will see others doing it and you might want to think about starting one up for yourself. In my previous book, *Creative Cosplay*, I broke down all the social media channels and their benefits for cosplayers. Each channel has its pros and cons, but there are more than just Facebook and TikTok.

COSPLAYERS: From left to right, April Gloria and Jedimanda
COSTUMES: From left to right, Magik and Doctor Strange from Marvel Cinematic Universe

Promote Yourself!

If you are interested in promoting yourself as a cosplayer and maybe expanding into a professional route, keep in mind that there are so many "professional" routes for people who cosplay. I consider anyone who gets paid for a gig or job to be a professional cosplayer. I consider myself a professional cosplayer. I guest at conventions, judge competitions, and write books about cosplay. Some cosplayers stream online for a living, have a model fan page, and/or make videos for money, which are all valid professional cosplay routes. But to make money, you do need to market yourself to companies or a public audience. The first step is to establish an audience for yourself online. The internet is the easiest and the number one way that companies or people find professional cosplayers. Sometimes, word of mouth and referrals from friends can help you get gigs without having a social media presence, but I think you should still consider establishing yourself online. Creating your cosplay name and then establishing profiles and an audience of fans are the first steps. If you want to go further, read on for a look into some of the options to help push yourself and your cosplay work in front of folks looking to hire.

VOLUNTEERING

Volunteering is a great way to start feeling more comfortable with people and larger audiences! At the beginning of my cosplay career, I started volunteering at public gatherings, hospital visits, or private events in costume. Surprisingly, there is a lot of work for event cosplay characters in hospitals to help cheer up the patients. Both types of volunteering are heartwarming and can bring such joy to the people you are there to entertain. Many cities and towns have charity groups or actual costuming groups (like the 501st Legion Star Wars fandom group) that have already been established to do this. Getting your feet wet with volunteer positions will help you make friends and connections, which will lead to more work and more opportunities to expand your profile in costuming. You can also volunteer at conventions to meet convention organizers and promote yourself, especially if you want to dive into the guesting game.

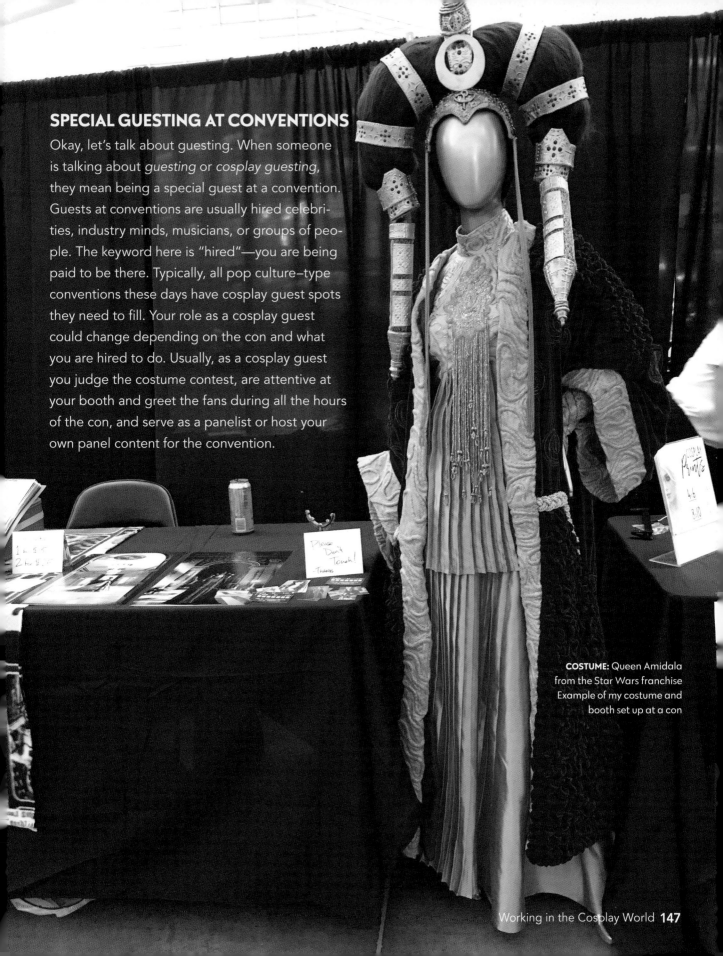

SPECIAL GUESTING AT CONVENTIONS

Okay, let's talk about guesting. When someone is talking about *guesting* or *cosplay guesting*, they mean being a special guest at a convention. Guests at conventions are usually hired celebrities, industry minds, musicians, or groups of people. The keyword here is "hired"—you are being paid to be there. Typically, all pop culture–type conventions these days have cosplay guest spots they need to fill. Your role as a cosplay guest could change depending on the con and what you are hired to do. Usually, as a cosplay guest you judge the costume contest, are attentive at your booth and greet the fans during all the hours of the con, and serve as a panelist or host your own panel content for the convention.

COSTUME: Queen Amidala from the Star Wars franchise Example of my costume and booth set up at a con

Being a cosplay guest at a convention is a pretty cool gig, I'm not going to lie. I've guested many times and have always thoroughly enjoyed it, but it's tough work. It's more than just sitting, smiling, and looking good in costume. It's also a pretty big honor to be a guest at a convention, and it comes with promotion and media on behalf of the convention. Your name will be out there—in programs, on social media, and in front of hundreds or thousands of future fans. Getting these positions can be tricky. Sometimes it's about who you know and have worked with; other times, conventions ask people to apply and choose guests from the applicants.

As a cosplay guest, you are expected to do a lot, so be prepared to fly by the seat of your pants. If you are contacted to be a guest, request payment! You are giving hours of your time to a convention where guests are paid to be there, so you should be paid too. You and your time are valuable; don't doubt yourself when pitching a rate. This may make you uncomfortable, even if it's not your first time guesting. Don't be afraid to ask other cosplayer guests what they charge. We are a community, and we help each other. Now that you have a good idea of what it takes to guest, it's time to create a media kit.

Either way, if you are chosen to be a cosplay guest at a convention, you need to remember several things:

- Be professional during all hours of the convention

- Show up on time

- Prepare to meet and greet lots of fans

- Treat everyone with respect

- Prepare to possibly be on camera

- Be at your booth as much as you can

- Stay hydrated and eat to keep your energy up

- Keep change at your booth if dealing with money

- Be prepared for anything that can be brought to you, from TV interviews to a surprise happy birthday photo. Just know that guesting can entail more than you think.

Trying to get that lunch during a convention is harder than it seems.

Me dressed as Captain Marvel interacting with children at a convention.

How to Make a Media Kit

A media kit is a document you create to display information about yourself, your skills, and sometimes your pay rate. These are insanely helpful to have on hand to send to companies, conventions, and anyone wanting to hire you for a gig. They explain who you are and what you have to offer, and you certainly should include a good bit of bragging. Some cosplayers include their pay rate for the tasks they are being asked to do. I include rates for sponsored posts within my social media, and I usually ask the hiring person to contact me directly, via email, to discuss terms for guesting spots. Get creative with the look of your media kit so it displays your personality.

One of the best places to create a media kit is through Canva. Signing up for Canva gives you access to tons of templates to help get you started. Include your favorite photos of you in your cosplays and write a great bio about yourself. I recommend adding social media follower counts and/or a list of the social media channels where you have a presence. Then finish up with your contact information and pay rates for the types of tasks or items for which you want to promote yourself. After you are finished, keep a PDF copy on a cloud-based server so you can send it out anytime and/or provide a link on your website for a digital download. Don't forget to keep revising your media kit by adding awards and recognitions, published works, collaborations, and follower counts.

COSPLAYER | INFLUENCER | FANDOM GURU

JEDIMANDA

MEDIA KIT

AMANDA H.

Professionally working in costuming since 2008. Amanda has done sewing/costuming work from professional theatre to bridal parties. Tired with creating beautiful creations for ballerinas and actors, she dove into cosplay head first in 2012. Within a year, she was already drawing big wins within the cosplay competition community. She continues to travel nationwide with her costumes to compete and meet her fans! Posting to social media multiple times daily, her audience grows with each tutorial, and work in progress post. Amanda won't stop competing and teaching until she becomes one with her sewing machine.

STATISTICS

60K	11	30K
Total social media followers	Cosplay competition awards won	Website hits

SOCIAL MEDIA FOLLOWING

| 25.6K | 11K | 18K | 5.5K |

INFLUENCER POST RATES

——— flat rate for static posts on Instagram (story and wall), Facebook, and Twitter. Rates vary for Youtube sponsored video, please contact Amanda for further discussion.

CONTACT ME

Jedimanda@gmail.com
www.jedimanda.com

Websites

Establishing your own website is one of the first things you need to do if you want to pursue a career in cosplay. In my opinion, the main reason to establish a website is to enable companies and groups to find your portfolio, view your media kit, and to contact you. If they want to hire you for a gig, this is where most people start looking. WordPress, Squarespace, Wix, and GoDaddy are websites with premade templates to help you establish a site. Once you create a basic site, I recommend filling it with content that helps you promote yourself. If you are big into video content and make a lot of tutorials, put a section on your site with your videos. Do you sell patterns, tutorials, or costumes? Put a section about that on your site. The must-have tabs on your website should be your cosplay portfolio, your bio (sometimes called About Me), and a contact tab so readers can communicate with you. Customize your site and make it feel like you!

Other Ideas to Help Promote Your Cosplay Career

Other than guesting, there are many options to pursue in launching a cosplay career. Giving workshops or being part of a panel at a convention is always an option. Cosplay panels are a part of conventions that help fill out the programming. Many convention attendees take advantage of the opportunity to learn something new and attend these panels. They are lots of fun, and the people on the panels are very knowledgeable. If you feel confident about an aspect of cosplay, consider teaching a workshop or giving a panel talk.

In a workshop, attendees usually create something tangible or do a hands-on activity. Workshops require you to provide the activity, machines, tools, or materials to help complete the task. Most workshops require attendees to pay to sign up and attend, so make sure you are compensated.

A panel talk is a lecture or a Q and A session. For a panel, you will likely need to make a presentation or some kind of digital video component. Keeping your audience engaged while you are talking is key. The worst thing is if people get up and leave during your panel, potentially leaving your room empty. Keeping them engaged with your topic will keep their butts in their seats.

These are great ways to get your name out there and in good standing with the convention committee to help further your cosplay career.

A typical panel setup at a convention.

COSPLAYER: Jedimanda
COSTUME: Yennefer of Vengerberg
from *The Witcher*

Final Thoughts

Besides conventions, creating online content is a great way to put your name out there. But social media is sometimes a lawless land, and you need to understand what and how you are putting yourself out there. Know when enough is enough. Escapism within cosplay is possible, but sometimes we can harm our mental health with the amount we post and expose ourselves to. In my first book, *Creative Cosplay*, I dive deeper into the psychology and escapism that cosplay can bring you. I want to specify here that if you choose to jump into the professional cosplay career world, you better be ready to work hard. Cosplay, even if it seems mainstream, it's still niche. Not everyone knows our capabilities or what cosplay can bring to the masses. Prepare your mind, body, and sewing machine for a tough but rewarding world.

COSPLAYER: Jedimanda
COSTUME: Lydia Deetz from *Beetlejuice*

INTERVIEW WITH GINNY DI

I would like to introduce you all to Ginny Di, a professional cosplayer, YouTuber, singer, and one of the hardest working people I know. She has put her mind, body, and soul into her career and developed into one of the most iconic content creators online now. I interviewed Ginny to pick her brain about cosplay marketing, professionalism online and at conventions, finding your niche, and choosing cosplaying as a career. Let's have a chat!

Can you give a brief background on yourself and your path to becoming a full-time content creator and professional cosplayer?

I spent most of my life planning on pursuing a career as either a writer or a teacher, but I had always loved costumes, creative play, and performing, so cosplay came very naturally to me. I sort of stumbled into some luck as a hobbyist: My Arya Stark, from *Game of Thrones*, cosplay took off due to the sheer chance of having a face that resembled the actress, Maisie Williams, and I also made some YouTube videos with friends that a lot of people followed. So when I was struggling to find a foothold in the professional cosplay world after graduating college, the online space was where I was succeeding. I started pursuing it more seriously as an outlet while working jobs I wasn't passionate about, and eventually, my cosplay world grew to the point where I knew I couldn't grow it any further without really dedicating myself to it. So I quit my job and took the plunge! That was in 2017, and I'm still a full-time internet person today.

COSPLAYER: Ginny Di
COSTUME: Arya from *Game of Thrones*
Photo by Ginny Di

What was the defining moment that made you turn to creating cosplay content full time?

I remember there was a morning when I woke up at five in the morning and got into my Ciri costume from *The Witcher* to shoot some sunrise photos before I had to be at work. It was the only time all week that I could squeeze in a shoot, and I had a deadline because it was for Patreon rewards. I showed up at work with a red line on my face where the fake scar was, having just scrubbed off my makeup fifteen minutes before, completely exhausted, and I thought, "This isn't sustainable."

I'd spent the previous year actively working toward building a business, although at the time I still thought of it as a side hustle. But I had reached the point where either work was getting in the way of cosplay, or cosplay was getting in the way of work. So I sat down and started looking at finances. That's when I realized I was already making nearly enough to cover my base living expenses. I turned in my two weeks' notice shortly after.

You and your admin team have developed the Cosplay Marketing Facebook group, and it has grown to almost 4,000 members! Why did you create a marketing group just for cosplayers?

Back when I created that group in 2015, I was really interested in learning to apply marketing strategy to my creative work, but bringing that kind of thing up in your average cosplay space drew a lot of judgment, and general marketing groups often felt either irrelevant or out of reach for my own work. I created the group as a place where cosplayers could ask each other things like "What hashtags have been good for you on Instagram?" or "Do you have any tips for reaching more people on Twitter?" and talk with like-minded cosplayers who are also trying to grow their following. I'm so proud to say that it's grown into a truly amazing community space where cosplayers share their insights, questions, and techniques every day!

COSPLAYER: Ginny Di
COSTUME: Tasha from *Dungeons & Dragons*
Photo by Ginny Di

What's your biggest marketing tip to cosplayers wanting to expand their careers into the professional cosplay world?

This is a bit of a "tough love" tip, but I think it's a really important thing to learn up front: Nobody owes you attention! Even if you work really hard, even if you do everything right, people will only engage with your work if it does something for them—makes them feel something, entertains them, educates them, inspires them. I see so many cosplayers who seem to think that if they put enough sweat in, they deserve success, but that's just not how entertainment works. The bottom line is this: The cosplayers who succeed are the ones who create work that people want to see. That should always be part of your strategy if you want to pursue cosplay professionally.

Cosplay guesting at conventions is such a big part of being a professional cosplayer; do you have any advice for first-time cosplay guests?

COSPLAYER: Ginny Di
COSTUME: Jester from *Critical Role*
Photo by Ginny Di

Honestly, my biggest guesting tip is to remember that you don't have to do it! Personally, as a socially anxious introvert, I find convention guesting really draining. So I don't do it much! I think there's an expectation that guesting is a necessary or even central part of a pro cosplayer's job, and even though for many cosplayers it is, you can build your business on whatever parts of cosplay are most compelling to you.

Over the years, you have blossomed within the tabletop gaming community. Would you say finding a niche fandom or skill set is ideal in continuing to be a full-time content creator?

There's a lot of talk about "finding a niche" in marketing creative work, and while I don't disagree that it can be really lucrative, I think hunting for it is often unsuccessful. I spent years trying to form a niche for myself and never really gaining ground, but when I organically fell in love with tabletop gaming, things just started coming together. If you feel like you're trying to force it and not having success developing a focus as a creator, my best tip is just to step back and let yourself follow the things that are exciting to you. Passion is visible in creative work, and when you're really energized about something, your viewers will be able to feel that energy!

Being a full-time content creator is so hard! How do you keep it all together?

The key to surviving being a full-time content creator is strict boundary setting! Self-employment is hard as it is, and being your own "product" makes it even harder. Without proper boundaries, I make myself miserable reading all of the things people say about me on social media. I work 80-hour weeks and skip weekends. I set totally unrealistic expectations. I find it can be helpful to ask myself, "If a boss were making me do all this, would that be a healthy employment situation?" And if the answer is no, I try to make a change. I'm not going to pretend I have it all under control, but I'm always learning better ways to handle it.

How do you see the world of professional cosplaying growing in the future?

I already feel like it's so different than it was just five or ten years ago! The biggest change I've seen, which I think will continue, is that cosplay is more accessible than ever before. That's great news for hobbyists, but it's a challenge for aspiring pros. It's harder and harder to stand out in a marketplace this crowded. To be totally honest, I don't know if I believe that "professional cosplay" on its own will continue to be a job—or if it is one now!

I used to call myself a pro cosplayer, but now I refer to myself as a YouTuber, because that's where most of my income comes from. Other cosplayers make their money from designing and selling patterns or books or fabrics, taking commissions, or streaming gaming on Twitch. The world where you could make a living solely by making and wearing costumes is disappearing or maybe is already gone. Instead, everyone has to figure out which combination of content creation they want to do, with cosplay being one facet, and others being YouTube, Twitch, commissions, podcasts, appearances, merch, and so on.

Ultimately, I think this is exciting! I see so much more diversity in the ways that cosplayers are embracing their craft these days. The fact that I can combine cosplay with singing while one friend combines cosplay with fitness and another friend combines it with science is just incredible! In a hobby where we are often making the exact same costumes as other people and striving to look exactly the same, I think it's a great opportunity to show off what makes us special and unique.

Thanks for letting me interview you, Ginny! Tell us a fun fact about yourself.

In elementary school, I wrote and distributed a weekly newsletter to my neighbors during the summer called *Ginny's Gazette*. (In case you needed more proof that I'm a huge nerd.)

Where can people follow Ginny Di?

YOUTUBE: youtube.com/ginnydi

TWITTER: twitter.com/itsginnydi

INSTAGRAM: instagram.com/itsginnydi

PATREON: patreon.com/ginnydi

WEBSITE: ginnydi.com

COSPLAYER: Ginny Di
COSTUME: Ciri from
The Witcher
Photo by Ginny Di

RESOURCES

Creative Cosplay:
Selecting & Sewing
Costumes Way Beyond
Basic, by Amanda
Haas offers up all the
information you need to
get sewing on your first or
your first few cosplays!

The Art of Extreme Wig
Styling, by Regan Cerato
is an in-depth look at
creating custom wigs to
go with any costume.

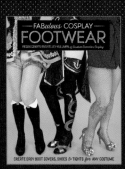

Fabulous Cosplay
Footwear: Create Easy
Boot Covers, Shoes &
Tights for Any Costume,
by Regan Cerato & Kelley
Kullman takes the hassle
out of finding the right
shoes, boots, and cosplay
legwear.

Smocking Secrets: 20
Stitch Patterns to Create
Unforgettable Texture;
Cosplay, Garment, Home
Decor & More, by Maggie
Hofmann shows you
how to create amazing
textures and visual
effects with just fabric,
needle, and thread.

Smocking Stencils:
Foolproof Templates to
Create Amazing Texture
for Cosplay, Garment &
Home Dec Sewing, by
Maggie Hofmann make
smocking even easier
and ensure your stitches
are evenly spaced for
perfect results.

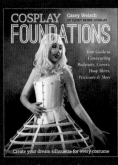

Cosplay Foundations:
Your Guide to
Constructing Bodysuits,
Corsets, Hoop Skirts,
Petticoats & More, by
Casey Welsch gives you
all the instruction you
need to get the perfect
silhouette for everything
from a ballgown to an
armored costume.

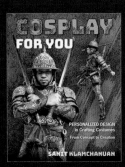

Cosplay for You:
Personalized Design in
Crafting Costumes; From
Concept to Creation,
by Sanit Klamchanuan
shows how tacking
original designs is both
completely possible and
amazingly fulfilling.

The Cosplay Book of
Ballgowns: A Complete
Guide to Creating Your
Own Masterpiece, by
Regan Cerato and Kelley
Kullman of Cowbutt
Crunchies Cosplay opens
the door to whipping
up the ballgown of your
dreams without the
headaches.

Cosplay Fabric FX:
Painting, Dyeing &
Weathering Costumes
Like a Pro, by Julianna
Franchini is the perfect
guide to creating
special effects on fabric
including age, dirt, blood,
and much more.

Cosplayer's Ultimate
Guide to EVA Foam:
Design, Pattern & Create;
Level Up Your Costumes &
Props, by Beverly Downen
takes the mystery out
of working with EVA
foam. Learn how to craft
costumes, props, and
more with this amazingly
versatile material.

ABOUT THE AUTHOR

As a professional seamstress, author, and avid costume maker with more than nine years of experience, Jedimanda has competed in—and ultimately won—several costume competitions and judged about the same amount. She has been featured in *Star Wars Insider* and *Cosplay Culture* Magazine, as well as on websites such as StarWars.com, D23 (the Disney fan club), Kotaku, Nerdist, Marvel.com and SyFy. Jedimanda loves to pour her heart and soul into cosplays, with a distinctive eye for accuracy, originality, and just plain fun. She loves to travel all across the United States for competitions, meet fans, teach cosplay panels, and genuinely interact with nerds like her.

She tries to divide her time between her love of costume making, painting, bread making, and building her SFX makeup portfolio with enough time to pet her black cat, Salem. She has a BFA in fine art painting from the University of Louisville. She split most of her time during and after college between working in theater with costume shop duties and getting her feet wet in the cosplay industry.

Online, Amanda is an admin for the SheProp community on Facebook. SheProp is a forum for those who self-identify as female, nonbinary, or trans propmakers, costume designers, SFX artists, cosplayers, and more, at all skill levels, to get together and chat about all things cosplay.

When she's not sewing her eyeballs out, she is the marketing and communications coordinator at the Speed Art Museum in Louisville, Kentucky.

Cosplayer's Ultimate Guide to Eva Foam

Fabulous Cosplay Footwear

Creative Cosplay

Fabulous Cosplay Footwear

The Art of Extreme Wig Styling

The Art of Extreme Wig Styling

Creative Cosplay

The Art of Extreme Wig Styling

The Cosplay Book of Ballgowns

FanPowered PRESS

Developed with our cosplay authors, FanPowered Press evokes how C&T's authors inspire and expand crafting topics by presenting innovative methods and ideas. We hope to inspire you to jump into something new and get outside of your comfort zone!

Want more creative content? Visit us online at **ctpub.com**